# Different Drums

'If a man does not keep in step with his fellows it may be because he hears a different drummer.'

THOREAU

# DIFFERENT DRUMS

### A Doctor's Forty Years in Eastern Africa

## Michael Wood

## Photographs by David Coulson

## Clarkson N. Potter, Inc./Publishers

DISTRIBUTED BY CROWN PUBLISHERS, INC., NEW YORK

Published in the United States by Clarkson N.
Potter, Inc., 225 Park Avenue South, New York,
New York 10003

Originally published in Great Britain by Century
Hutchinson Ltd, Brookmount House, 62–65
Chandos Place, Covent Garden, London WC2N
4NW

(Title page) A big dust storm sweeps down the Great Rift Valley,
obliterating the landscape. Advancing along a 50-mile front, storms like
these can rise to a height of 30,000 feet or more above ground level.

(This page) Gabbra village on the move in the Chalbi Desert. Curved
poles from the dismantled huts are packed on the camels' backs.

CLARKSON N. POTTER, POTTER, and
colophon are trademarks of Clarkson N. Potter,

Manufactured in the Netherlands

Library of Congress Cataloging-in-
Publication Data
Wood, Michael, 1919–
  Different Drums.

  Includes index.
  1. Aeronautics in medicine—Kenya.
2. Aeronautics in medicine—Tanzania.
3. Wood, Michael, 1919–    . 4. Physicians—
Kenya—Biography. 5. Physicians—
Tanzania—Biography. 6. Folk medicine—
Kenya. 7. Folk medicine—Tanzania.
8. Medical care—Africa, East.   I. Title.
RA996.55.K4W66  1987    610′.92′4 [B]
87-2351
ISBN  0-517-56655-9

10 9 8 7 6 5 4 3 2 1

First American Edition

# Contents

# Acknowledgements

In writing this book I have had one outstanding helper, my wife. Not only has she shared many of my experiences and thoughts but she has found the phrases to express them which are woven into this book. Her commitment to Africa, her sympathy for the African cause and her faith in the future all find expression here.

The views set out in this book are my own and not necessarily those of any organization with which I have worked. It is an attempt to depict some of the events that have occurred over the last few decades as a result of the generosity of many organizations and people who have donated to the African Medical and Research Foundation. I would like to thank Adrian House for the help and encouragement he gave on the text in the early stages. David Coulson's photographs catch the beauty of the people and the country and I am greatly indebted to his skill, interest and involvement in the final product. I know the photographs will help those readers, who have not yet been able to visit Africa, to visualize some of the scenes described in the text.

Both David and I would also like to express our gratitude to Stephen Coe for his help and advice with the jacket concept.

M.W.

# Photographer's Note

My objective in this book has been to tell the visual story behind Michael Wood's text. Where possible I have tried to capture the atmosphere and mood of the places he describes, as well as the pathos or beauty of the people he has come to know. The project has been physically, technically and logistically challenging. It is not possible, for instance, to make a telephone appointment to photograph a witch-doctor at work. Numerous journeys may be required, involving hundreds of miles of difficult bush driving and when you get there he may be absent, or have no patients. There was also the time that I was photographing Michael operating on a man who had been flattened by a buffalo. Again and again I was forced to tie and retie my shoelaces between shots to prevent myself from passing out. For aerial photography we would take off the right-hand door of the aircraft to give me an uninterrupted view. On one occasion, as Michael banked sharply for me to photograph the crater of a volcano directly below, I noticed my seatbelt hanging loose and unattached from the open doorway. 'Thank God', we said, 'for centrifugal force.'

For interested photographers I should say that all the photographs in this book were taken on Kodachrome and Fujichrome film using Nikon 35 mm equipment. To begin with I used F2 cameras and a Nikormat EL but later changed to Nikon F3s. Most of the portraits in this book were taken with an 80 mm/200 mm zoom and many of the others with my 28 mm wideangle and 35–70 mm lenses. I used a motordrive and high-shutter speeds for the aerial photography.

I would like to mention my own appreciation to AMREF for all the support they have given me during this project. Without their help many of the photographs would have been difficult or impossible to obtain. In particular I should like to thank Nyambura Githagui, Anne Spoerry, Nicky Blundel-Brown, Jim Heatherhayes, Liz Young and Calum MacPherson for all their help and kindness. Apart from AMREF, there were also others who went out of their way to help me, and in particular I should like to thank Ahmed Sheikh Nabahani and Fabby Nielson in Mombasa, Worku Sharew in Ethiopia, Michael Keating (p. 128) and Susannah Hallauer for their photographs (pp. 125 and 127), Eva Monley, Cecilia Kershaw, Richard Nightingale and my parents.

Perhaps my greatest debt, however, is to Angela Fisher and Carol Beckwith with whom I have worked so closely in the last few years and who have also contributed photographs (Angela pp. 42 and 80 and Carol p. 86 [top]). Lastly I too should like to thank Susan Wood for her special contribution to this book, and Michael himself for leading me into a field of endless fascination.

D.C.

# A Forethought

**M**odern Africa is a new phenomenon in the world. It presents new problems as it grows in strength and form. A synthesis of a very old culture and an overlay of a western-style civilization is taking place with surprising results. Sitting, surrounded by comfortable modern accoutrements, and looking out on the wild hills of old Africa I am aware of these presences, both traditional and western, and the new Africa which is developing from their meeting.

I have lived in Africa for forty years and during that time have seen rapid changes, and in the course of my medical work have been able to bridge some gaps of understanding. I came to Africa immediately after the Second World War to act as assistant to a surgeon whose practice had grown enormously with the war. My wife, Susan, and our two small children came with me. We expected to stay six months and have stayed for our lifetime so far. My surgical practice was varied, and in 1955 I did a further postgraduate course in reconstructive surgery to handle the amount of trauma and burns needing treatment. Susan and I had two more children in Africa and, through her parents who came to the continent as missionaries during the First World War, our grandchildren are now fifth generation 'African' and as a family we are rooted in African soil.

As we continued to live in Nairobi, I found myself longing to be part of native Africa and not to remain simply a town dweller. We moved, therefore, to live on a farm twenty miles out of Nairobi, and later from there to larger farms on Kilimanjaro. The greatest reward that I have had from farming in Africa is a sense of sharing that most essential of African experiences, the struggle to produce a livelihood from the soil.

By the time we took up farming on Kilimanjaro I had learnt to fly, and commuted at the weekends to the farm. I also learnt that flying could revolutionize the spread and quality of modern medicine in Africa. By using modern communications, both air and radio, the small amount of money available for health services in Africa could be made to take specialist services to the bush hospitals, to carry patients to hospital centres, and to give advice and encouragement to those dealing with problems far out in the bush. This led to the start of the Flying Doctor Service, which was the first operation of the African Medical and Research Foundation – better known as AMREF – which now runs many medical projects in eastern Africa.

I have tried in this book to describe Africa as I see it today. Yet despite my long association with the country and its peoples, I remain conscious of my scientific training, my roots in European culture and a different race. Given these origins, my eyes necessarily cannot see the whole picture. My intuition tells me of other realities, other viewpoints and goals, and recognizes my inherent limitations. It is my hope that this strange mixture of insight and sight from outside will throw new light on Africa's path into the future.

**THE MAPS** on the following pages are of Kenya, Sudan and Ethiopia. The last two relate particularly to Chapters 9 and 10 respectively.

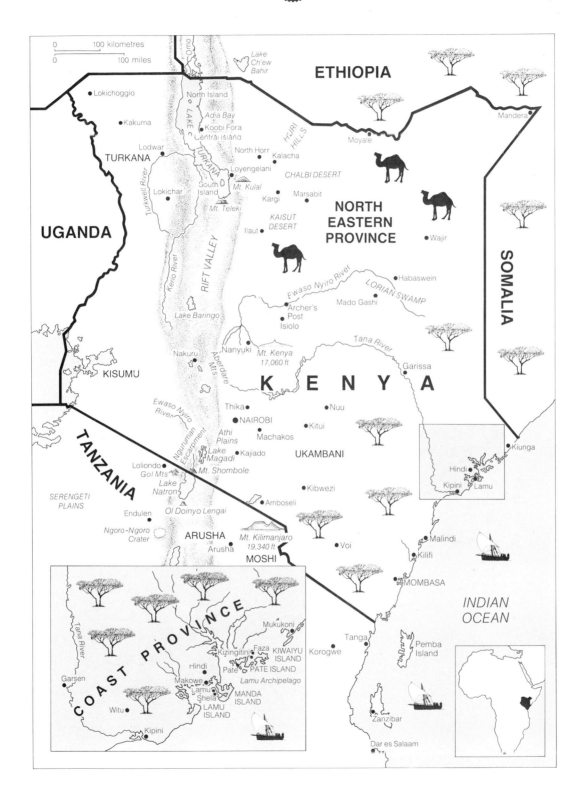

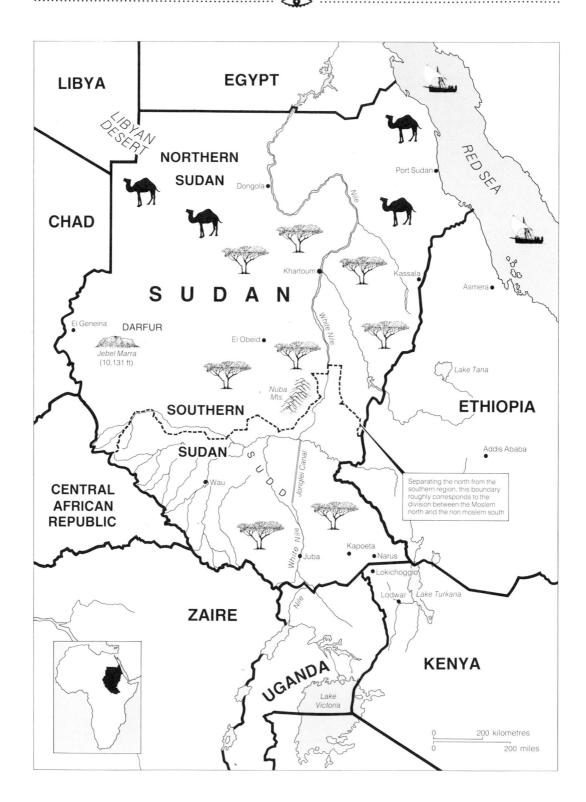

LIBYA

EGYPT

LIBYAN DESERT

NORTHERN
SUDAN

CHAD

Dongola

Port Sudan

RED SEA

Nile

S U D A N

Khartoum

Kassala

Asmera

El Geneina

DARFUR

Jebel Marra
(10,131 ft)

El Obeid

White Nile

Nuba
Mts.

Lake Tana

ETHIOPIA

SOUTHERN

SUDAN

S
U
D
D

Jonglei Canal

Addis Ababa

CENTRAL
AFRICAN
REPUBLIC

Wau

Separating the north from the
southern region, this boundary
roughly corresponds to the
division between the Moslem
north and the non moslem south

White Nile

Kapoeta

Juba

Narus

Lokichoggio

Lodwar

Lake Turkana

ZAIRE

Nile

KENYA

UGANDA

Lake
Victoria

0          200 kilometres

0          200 miles

SUDAN

RED SEA

YEMEN

Kassala

Asmara

ERITREA

Axum

*Danakil*
*Depression*

TIGRE

Gonder

WALO

*Lake Tana*

Lalibela

Dessie

FRENCH
SOMALILAND

Djibouti

GULF OF ADEN

Bahir Dar

*Blue Nile*

SOMALIA

Herar

ADDIS ABABA

ETHIOPIA

OGADEN

*Bale Mts.*

SOUTHERN
SUDAN

*RIFT VALLEY*

*Lake*
*Turkana*

UGANDA

Loyangalani

SOMALIA

KENYA

0          200 kilometres
0          200 miles

*Blue Nile*

11

# CHAPTER ONE

# AN OLD DRUM BEAT

T he old Land Rover came to a halt in a cloud of dust. Everyone sat still waiting for it to subside. The occupants of the vehicle shifted restlessly, all too well aware of the sweat and dust that clung uncomfortably to their skins. No one spoke for a while, as the noise of the Land Rover was silenced, and the heat of the afternoon hammered down on the iron roof.

A group of thorn trees off the road gave thin shade and the small company made for it thankfully, eager to escape from the burning sun. The air smelt strongly of goats and cattle, and a hot wind moved the sand in a desultory fashion at their feet. A small dust-devil whirled past throwing the pungent grit into their faces as they set off up a small hill to visit Bengei – a witchdoctor or healer, depending on which way you chose to look at it.

Bengei enjoyed considerable fame as a healer of mental disturbances, and they had come to witness his famous treatment for madness, which consisted of burying a patient alive for one hour. To assist the cure the patient was to be buried with a goat, which would attract the evil spirit out of the mad person, and die as a result, while the patient would be resuscitated and live.

At the top of the hill was a small entrance to what looked like a cave. Huge granite boulders marked the doorway. It was surrounded by heavy bushes and a gnarled old tree grew out of one side casting shade over the entrance. The whole place was cool, shrouded in trees and shadow, and the party began to recover their breath, and enjoy some relief from the great heat of the road and sparsely grassed plains below.

Bengei stood at the entrance, a tall man with dark, kindly eyes that sparkled with vitality and lent him an air of authority. He explained that when entering this holy place everyone should enter backwards, men putting forward their right foot first and women the left. Inside it was hushed and cool, a place in which to remain quiet, to save questions for another time and place. As the light from the entrance began to fill the chamber, unidentifiable bones hanging in clusters round the room came into focus. On the floor stood gourds of unnamed potions, whose secret rested with this man and his young son whom he seemed to be instructing in his knowledge.

Silence enveloped the party like a velvet curtain. No one dared, or even cared, to speak. The musty air smelt of bats and unspeakable concoctions. After a pause Bengei spoke. He explained that the patient and the site chosen for the treatment were some way away. The treatment itself would not take place until arrangements had been completed for the purchase of a goat and the settlement of a fee. Bengei then requested the party to follow him after a pause for resting. After about half an hour he gave the sign to move and, strangely refreshed, the party moved together down the hill.

A short walk brought them to a grove of trees. The red earth was bare of grass and around the grove were many mounds of soil, like old graves, where previous patients had received his treatment. To the largest tree a woman was tied, looking about her with an animal fear on her face and madness in her eyes. Beneath another tree a group of relatives was busy haggling over the price of the goat. The prepared grave was about four feet deep and, as the group stood round, Bengei outlined the procedure for the treatment. All were welcome to attend, he said, but it could be

complete. Realising that the two days could easily turn into weeks, the party reluctantly took their leave. The events that followed were later graphically described to David Coulson by Bengei's wife when David returned some months later in order to discover the fate of the mad woman.

*The men bound the patient hand and foot, lowered her into the grave and covered her head and face with a sack. The goat was likewise bound and lowered beside her into the grave. The woman now lay still, while the goat struggled hopelessly to get free. The men began to shovel the earth on top of the pair, and soon two feet of earth held them captive. A fire was then prepared on top of the grave. The wood caught easily and the flames shot high into the hot air. The people round waited in a small stunned group sitting the hour out in awkward silence. The relatives brooded sullenly on the far side of the grave and Bengei sat by himself as if in a trance.*

*At the appropriate moment Bengei rose and gave the signal for the exhumation. The earth was shovelled roughly aside and with surprising speed the bodies became visible. Both of them seemed lifeless. The goat was raised first and was indeed dead. The woman was then raised; she was unconscious but as Bengei massaged her and threw water on her face, she moved in a dazed fashion and slowly came back to life. It was impossible to say at that moment if she was cured in the instant, but she was quiet and neither struggled nor moaned, and no longer regarded us with that insane ferocity which she had previously shown. Her relatives helped her stumble away.*

.............................................

*(Opposite) Bengei specialized in curing people of mental illness and his treatment for this condition was live burial in pits like this. He is seen here standing over an assistant during the ritual preparations before burial.*

.............................................

*(Previous page) On the East African coast there is still a strong belief in spirits, both the good and the bad. A goat is being sacrificed as part of an exorcism ceremony, while the sun rises over the Indian Ocean. After being transferred from a sick man to the unfortunate goat, the evil spirit will now flow out into the sea with the goat's lifeblood, washed away on the tide. Many of the worst Shetani (evil spirits) are thought to come from the sea.*

*A patient has been brought in to be treated by Bengei. She is tied by her wrists to the base of a tree waiting to be buried alive. We later learnt that the treatment had been completely successful. She had made a full recovery.*

As David related this remarkable story I remember questioning in my own mind whether such a treatment could be akin to our electrical shock treatment of mentally deranged patients. Could the shock, or the lack of oxygen in the brain, cause some change in the brain cells themselves? I played with scientific answers but none held. I was left with the knowledge that these were causes and effects from another world; another reality existed alongside mine with different answers, different methods, which were beyond my comprehension yet were none the less valid.

The subject of traditional medicine has been uppermost in my mind for years and I have increasingly come to understand its importance in relation to western scientific medicine. As a Western-trained doctor I was initially sceptical of the subject, but gradually learnt to differentiate between the genuine and the bogus. Some understanding of traditional medicine is essential if one is to see where scientific medicine can complement it and where, of course, the converse applies. For a brief interval I had entered Africa's spirit world, which is so close to the African and which we, with our tradition of scientific understanding and 'logic', with our devotion to cause and effect, can only dimly sense.

The new physics which begins to open up for us a new dimension of existence, revealing waves which continue for ever, vibrations which do not peter out but can be recorded long after, humanly speaking, they are finished, finds an echo in the primal vision of a world inhabited by the spirits of the dead, who continue to

16

influence subsequent generations. In this view of the world things do not happen by chance. Every event is the conscious intention of some person or spirit. The soul of a man is spread over his relatives alive or dead, and even over his possessions; thus inanimate things are imbued with a spirit and life of their own. Prayers are said to the ancestors most recently dead, since they are nearest to earth. The longer an ancestor has been dead the more revered he is, for he is nearest to the Great Spirit who broods over all.

How far we of the materialist world have wandered from this earth-child concept, which could bring us back to a new love and care for our environment, where the animals, plants and insects of the earth are seen again as our companions in life, indeed as a very extension of ourselves.

On his return visit to Bengei, David found to his amazement that the great healer who was not old or ailing, had died. The circumstances of his death were related by his widow and the villagers.

It was a curious story. The villagers said that a neighbouring witch had been envious of some of Bengei's land. He had withstood every pressure to sell it to her, until one day a huge snake appeared on his doorstep. Bengei took a panga and slew the snake. The villagers immediately became alarmed for Bengei, for they felt that the snake had certainly been sent by the witch. Bengei was indifferent to their pleas that he kill a goat on the spot where he had killed the snake, for he felt confident in his own magic. That same day he had been bitten by a tick and although he had been taken to hospital and Nairobi experts had been consulted, he had swelled up all over his body, and finally even the doctors agreed that it was witchcraft. By the end of the week he was dead. David records:

*The widow took me up to his special room below the big granite boulder. As I followed her up the winding path a small hand took mine firmly in its grasp and I looked down into two large eyes set in a little replica of Bengei's face. Somehow that thirteen-year-old boy had sensed my sadness and interest, and a natural sympathy passed between us. I had liked Bengei and, though poles apart, we had experienced a brief rapport. At the entrance I took off my shoes and entered backwards as was customary. Nothing had changed since his death – the tall carved figure standing like an altarpiece at one end, the hole in the floor from which the python used to emerge when bidden, the huge cow horn containing the powerful magic of plants, animal teeth, porcupine quills, human parts, hyena excreta still standing in its place ready to be placed across the door to prevent entry. The place was awe-full and eerie.*

David stood there in silence contemplating this extraordinary sequence of events. Where did psychology end and witchcraft begin? Could it have been called poison or the work of the supernatural? Had it been fear that had overcome Bengei's confidence and apparent strength? What was reality for one person could be mumbo jumbo for another. Clearly reality for the villagers was very different from what David recognized as reality.

This presence of two realities, side by side, intrigues and challenges the stranger in Africa. It is the presence of this second reality which has caused the alien reality of the West to fail to take root, or where it has done so to produce unexpected and strange fruit. Colonial governments have largely ignored it, though individuals working in rural areas have come to acknowledge it and work alongside it. Today the course of events often rides rough-shod over these ancient realities, but it is at a cost that we ignore their validity for the vast majority of Africa's inhabitants.

Over the years the title of witchdoctor has been applied indiscriminately to the spiritual men of Africa, but nowadays they can be more carefully defined. Most basic of all are the traditional birth attendants, gnarled and knotted as old trees, who have acquired immense experience attending the numerous confinements in the rural areas and nomadic parts of Africa. They have little or no idea of hygiene and readily turn to magic when in difficulties, but they are a section of traditional doctoring which could easily form part of modern medical care if given instruction in hygiene and some basic procedures.

Other divisions of the so-called 'witchdoctor' profession are likewise akin to western science. The bonesetters of Africa have a well-earned reputation for skill, and with teaching could also form an extension of our present medical services. There are even surgeons in Kisii country who perform craniotomies for severe headache and have achieved considerable success by this method, some patients returning several times for this operation.

The men who perform these operations are called 'omobaris' and are highly skilled. They use no anaesthetic, but make use of herbs to clean the area of the frontal bone of the skull before making an incision with an ordinary knife or a hacksaw blade. The purpose of the operation is to relieve pressure by taking out a small section of the skull. The scalp is scraped off the bone with an old knife and then with a primitive trephine a section of the skull is cut out and removed. The skin is then left open to heal, being kept clean with herbs and a bunch of clean feathers. The omobari is so skilful that he can expose the pulsating dura without injuring it. This operation is said to be very ancient in origin, some holding that it actually derives from ancient Egypt.

On one occasion my daughter Katrina, who has made a study of traditional medicine, was present together with David Coulson at a 'bloodless' operation. A healer was called to deal with a woman who was reputed to have internal bleeding.

*This healer on the outskirts of Nairobi is boiling up roots from which he produces healing potions which are dispensed in bottles usually supplied by the patients. He is also a diviner, and has a thriving practice.*

*(Opposite) A Swahili herbalist identifies some of the ingredients of his trade. He explains how a combination of two particular herbs is a cure for asthma, and another combination a cure for malaria.*

She lay in his little mud house on a beautiful Persian carpet, which was kept specially for this use. He knelt beside her and placed a horn rather like a stethoscope to her abdomen, listening to a sound like surf on the shore. He then made a small incision with a razor blade, and placing his mouth to it, sucked with all his might. Finally, he removed something from his mouth and rubbed the incision with oil and herbs. Later he showed the object which he had removed from his mouth and which he claimed he had removed from the woman's abdomen. It was a curious stone-like object, which he said had been placed there by another witchdoctor on instructions from an enemy.

Herbalists are also a skilled and reputable section of African traditional medicine. Their profession is probably the easiest of all to assimilate into modern medicine and is most easily understood by our own practitioners. Some herbalists have a great knowledge of local plants and their uses and use them to great effect. They despatch people to all corners of the country to collect plants, and their knowledge along with its applications is kept very secret, and is only now becoming known. At a recent exhibition in Nairobi of herbalists and their medicines, I overheard one man in the crowd complaining, 'They do not have any potions to bring back a run-away wife, or to tell me how to get a job, or how to become rich!' Clearly the social problems of urban life are greater than the physical ones.

Even among the traditional herbalists many of them nowadays include in their apparatus things which pertain to modern science. It is as if they would impress their clients with their scientific techniques. The white coat and stethoscope are very popular and are frequently worn; nurses appear in uniform, while outside on the ground is an incongruous heap of herbs and roots being sorted through for administration to the patients who crowd the waiting room. Perhaps the most dangerous thing about the herbalists is their inability to measure dosage. A herb, which might have been a cure in the first place, can quickly turn killer if given in the wrong amount. They seem to have no accurate system of measuring their potions and science could help greatly in making their skills more effective.

Another class of witchdoctors are the diviners who with their inner sense of the unseen can find lost articles, discover the malice situated behind an accident, or diagnose the cause of an illness. Sometimes a diviner is also a healer and they are often used to advise on the source of trouble and outline the course of action to be taken. They are fascinating people with deep psychic powers, who often operate by going into a trance and gazing at stones, or by throwing a handful of bones in the dust to see how they fall. Sometimes the spirits of the ancestors are heard to speak through them, and they are held in great awe and esteem in the community.

*(Opposite above) Ritual mat used by a Nairobi healer for the treatment of spirit problems. The antelope horns represent different spirits and the cowrie shells spirits from the sea. The sides and corners of the bottom mat are raised to allow evil spirits to escape. In the background is a basket of gourds containing different potions.*

*(Opposite below) The same healer treats a girl who is suffering from spirit possession. It seems that the girl shares a husband with another wife and the latter has placed a curse on her. The white marks on the girl's skin were made with a particular chalk found only on mounts Kenya and Kilimanjaro. Under her yellow blanket the girl is holding a small child.*

But it is the great spirit healers who crown the achievements of African medicine. Not only can they diagnose an evil spirit but they command and communicate with him. In 'the drawing out of the spirit's heat', which is how spirit healers often describe what they do, one can see a likeness to a 'drawing out' of a mind's confusion by a psychiatrist. The spirit healer has within him the spiritual resources to deal with malevolent spirits and to bring calm and healing to a tormented mind, thus combining in himself the roles of the psychiatrist and priest of the western world.

Recently we were invited to visit a healer in the crowded confines of Nairobi itself. We wound our way down a narrow mud path between two hovels in a shanty town on the outskirts of the city. The district is known as Kibera and houses a great many of the office and industrial workers of the town. Situated on a rise overlooking Nairobi dam, it looks across at the wide expanse of the Athi Plains, whose great distances were softened in mist.

The house we were looking for faced onto a small open space and tiny shops

*At the coast, the seasons and all major events in life are controlled by spirits.*
*Most common of the spirits are the Jinis (Genies) who can be jealous, and*
*mischievous. In this illustration from* The Fisherman and the Genie *in*
Arabian Nights, *the Genie is seen appearing from a pot.*

were visible in the open doors opposite. As we walked, we gathered a small crowd of children in our train, who whistled and giggled at us, their eyes wide with curiosity. We knocked a little apprehensively on a door which was opened by a Mkamba woman, and we were ushered into the small dark room. She was a woman of medium height with a pale skin. Her face was oval with rounded features and her eyes were soft and shy. She spoke with confidence, however, asking us to sit against the wall of the house on a bench. She had been expecting us, as we had sent word ahead that we would like to come and photograph her practising her art of healing. We took our places quietly, not wanting to disturb the intent atmosphere of the proceedings.

22

As my eyes wandered round, taking in the small house and the strange artefacts which hung from the ceiling and walls, I pondered on the rift between African and Western thought concerning the cause of disease. It seemed to me the fundamental difference is that while we ask '*what* has caused my illness?' the African will ask '*who* is responsible for causing my illness?' In a world in which individual effort counts for little or nothing, when measured against the extreme fatalism which surrounds all events in Africa, people do not expect to take responsibility for their own health. Illness is either the result of someone else's malice, or it is the will of God. It is a personalized approach to a personal problem.

A young girl on a chair opposite me was the patient and beside her was her husband, a glum fellow, who avoided our greeting and nervously licked his lips. He told the healer that the girl was infertile, which is the worst fate that can befall a woman in Africa; it makes her life endlessly insecure. A man regards the procreation of children as the seal set on a marriage and even on his own immortality, and therefore a childless woman is easily disposed of and never attains any status in the community. The girl was dressed in a cotton slip of faded yellow. She wore a scarf round her head in the Kikuyu manner, and appeared unconcerned or indifferent to our appearance, as she sat sullenly looking at the floor.

*A Kamba diviner in Kibera (Nairobi) strums on her instrument (bow and gourd) to ascertain the nature of a patient's problems. Traditionally the Kamba were hunters, hence the use of the bow in these rituals. The Bible is used for the benefit of people who may have had a Christian education. The fee is paid in advance.*

*A coastal healer gives medicine to his patient following a bloodless operation to remove a 'foreign body' implanted by an ill-wisher. Note the gourd, below left, used for summoning spirits.*

Meanwhile the healer herself was busy placing an open Bible on a small table. On the Bible she placed a mirror and on the mirror she arranged a handful of stones. These were, it seemed, to be the sources of her inspiration. She then took a large Kamba hunting bow from the wall and, placing a gourd between the bowstring and the wood, began to strum out a rhythm. She closed her eyes, mumbling to herself, and appeared to go into a trance as she attempted to diagnose who was to blame for the patient's infertility. Suddenly she stopped her strumming and announced to the couple that it was another woman who had been the cause of this girl's problem. She then proceeded to call on the ancestors and the spirits to be merciful and to come and assist her with healing this patient.

After a while, as the silence built up in the hut and the atmosphere grew hotter, she left the table and, stripping the patient down to the waist, she began to wash her symbolically with a brush. Then from a gourd she poured a white ointment made from powdered roots into the palm of her hand and proceeded to anoint the patient's breasts. This done, she lit a torch made of goat's tail from the smouldering fire on the floor and waved it above the head of the girl, precariously near to her hair and eyes. The same procedure was followed as the girl lay on the floor and the torch was passed many times over her abdomen and incantations were said. As the treatment ended the patient began to look more relaxed. When we were about to leave, we noticed a smile on her face and wondered what the future held for this woman. Had something of deep psychological significance occurred, or were the medical explanations which leapt to mind, too serious to be allayed by purely mental resolution?

One of the most interesting things to me had been the use of the Bible as an instrument in calling up the spirits. It personified the dilemma in which so many people in Africa live today. The dichotomy between the modern age and ancient beliefs produces untold pressures in their lives. This girl had probably already been to the clinic at the Kenyatta Hospital, as well as consulting the local healer. It is better to appease the spirits, as well as trust in modern science.

The coastal area of Kenya is perhaps the area most alive with the sense of spirit life. Although it is in the main a strict Moslem part of the country, and no Moslem will admit to believing in the spirits, they nonetheless resort to spirit healers all the time. According to local belief there exists a realm of spirits over and above that of the ancestors. These are good and bad spirits who live alongside a good or bad man to keep him company. The very good spirits are called 'Rohanis' and the very bad spirits 'Shetanis'. There are also numerous 'Jinis' who are sometimes amiable but more often jealous and mischievous, though not as malicious as the Shetanis. People see most of their afflictions as originating from the ill will of one or other of these spirits, who has set upon them for some trifling misdemeanour or lack of respect.

One of the greatest spirit healers, known locally as Mwalimu or Teacher, lives in Mombasa, and David visited him in the course of his photography. He was a remarkable man, able to communicate with these antagonistic spirits, while using the words of the Koran to exorcise them. David witnessed one such session and wrote about it later.

*We watched him deal with a patient who had been suffering from fever and who had come to him after the hospital had failed to cure him. They had apparently treated him for malaria. This young man now sat with his family in Mwalimu's consulting room while we watched through the open window. Mwalimu's first task, as he explained to us, was to diagnose whether this was indeed malaria, or a mental problem, or whether it was a spiritual affliction. First of all he recited verses of the Koran over bottles of rosewater, blessing the water. Then he looked the patient in the eye and recited more verses from the Koran. This was his way of diagnosing the boy's problem. Whilst he didn't physically examine him, he could see where the problem lay. Later he explained to us that his Rohani helps him enormously with the diagnosis.*

*An antagonistic spirit was diagnosed to be the cause and he then called on the spirit to show its whereabouts. The patient at this point announced that he felt pressure at the top of his head and pointed to the spot. Mwalimu explained to us that the spirit had now shown itself and he was going to call it over to himself and see what the problem was. At that he placed both hands on the patient's head at the point where the patient had felt the pressure and called to the spirit in Arabic to come to him. At first there was silence and then suddenly Mwalimu convulsed and began to sneeze to the left and right. His eyes seemed to swim, and he murmured incoherently. Then, after two to three minutes, he returned to normal and said to us (in English), 'This is the situation. This boy has had a dispute with a friend of his uncle and the man has sent this spirit to attack him. I have told the spirit that I have come to mediate in this matter, and the spirit has agreed.' He then spoke to the boy in Swahili and asked him if there was anyone with whom he had had a dispute. The boy thought for a moment and then said, 'Yes, I have had trouble with a friend of my uncle's.' Mwalimu said, 'Yes, I know, and that is why you have this trouble because the man has sent a spirit to attack you. Now we shall ask the spirit to leave.' Once again Mwalimu went into a trance and a minute later he was back with us, saying that the spirit had now left the boy, who suddenly looked limp and exhausted. He gave the boy some holy rosewater to drink* and a couple of bottles to take away with him. 'Go away and rest,' he said.

The most dramatic case that Mwalimu related to us was of an occasion last year when he was called to the hospital to see a man who had been found in the branches of a tree, and who seemed to be out of his mind with fright. Mwalimu talked to him in the hospital and in a very short time became convinced that this was a bad case of bewitching.

He had the man brought to his house and talked to his relatives to see what they knew of the case. They seemed rather confused, but said that he had been mumbling something about a woman who had hit him and driven him through the town. This was all he had said and naturally they took this to be the ravings of someone who had gone off his head. The strange thing was that the police had found the man stripped and bruised high in the branches of a tree early one morning the previous week. How had he got there and why had he gone mad?

So Mwalimu recited his verses from the Koran and called to the Jini possessing this man to come to him. He felt the heat as the spirit came and he asked it to explain what was going on. He heard it reply 'like a telephone' in his head. 'I asked this man a simple question in the street – I asked him where the shop was – and he insults me unnecessarily saying, "Are you blind?" That is no way to talk to someone, whoever it is, and now he's being punished for his foolish rudeness. He knows that he must die and he has three choices for the manner of his death.' Once again Mwalimu explained to the Jini that he had come to mediate between the parties concerned and that since he was now involved there was no further reason for the Jini to continue his punishment. Reluctantly the Jini agreed to let Mwalimu settle the issue and then departed from the man, who recounted his experience.

He had met a young woman in the street, it seemed, on his way to the cinema. She had asked him where the nearest shop was and, since there was a shop only a few yards from where they both stood, which could not have been more obvious, he said to her, 'Are you blind?' At that she struck him across the face, sending him flying across the street. 'I knew it was impossible that this slip of a woman could be so strong, and I was frightened. As I picked myself from the gutter I saw her coming towards me and I ran as fast as I could down the street. I knew I had to get away, but when I looked back I saw her there behind me only a few yards away. Seconds later an iron hand grabbed my shoulder and I was thrown to the ground. I felt my shirt ripped from my body and somehow I got up again and ran away even faster, hoping I might meet someone who could help, then I heard a voice in my ears saying, "You only have three choices, foolish man. You may either hang yourself from a rope, or jump from a high cliff or, as a final alternative, drown yourself in the sea. You will die for the way you insulted me!" Then she threw me to the ground and my remaining clothes were torn from my body as one pulls leaves from a cob of corn. I ran on again, naked, her words ringing in my ears, and after that I can remember no more, except when those policemen were taking me down from the tree the next morning and I tried to talk but could not. They took me to the hospital and I was there until you came.'

Mwalimu gave the man three bottles of holy rosewater and advised him never again to go to that part of town, particularly at night. He told him that he would have to move to a different area where there was no chance of meeting this Jini again. He then asked the man's family to take him home to rest. Apparently he slept solidly for four days and since that time

A healer in Kibera (Nairobi) transfers an evil spirit from his patient into a black hen. The patient was suffering from swollen legs and only came to this healer after Western-trained doctors at three different hospitals had failed to help her. The white coat may be intended to give an air of respectability to the proceedings.

*has had no further trouble. Mwalimu has seen him several times and each time they recall the strange events that nearly ended in tragedy.*

*Jinis are reputed to live in big trees or holes in the ground. They sometimes take on animal forms such as dogs and are usually black. They can often be felt through heat, light or rumbling sounds. Rohanis can also turn nasty if their charge begins to sin against the Koran, and they are always frightening and awe-inspiring if they pay a man a visit.*

The seasons, and all major events in life, are controlled by spirits. At the coast before the great rains, cattle will sometimes be taken down to the water's edge and sacrificed at dawn to the rising sun. As their blood mingles with the white surf, prayers are said for the blessing of rain. All along the coast there exist caves in which prayers are still said to numerous malign or benevolent spirits. The priest or spirit healer stands in a shaft of light under a hole in the roof of the cave; lifting his arms in prayer he is bathed in soft light, and benefactions from the spirit world flow through him, bringing ordinary men and women hope.

The sorcerers, the real witchdoctors, are the last category of medicine men and they deal in spells and magic. Africa has long been held in thrall by them. A disgruntled neighbour, a jealous relative, in fact anyone with a grudge or envious of another man's wife, riches or good luck, can call upon the witchdoctor to cast a spell and no modern medicine can avail against such a disease. It can only be exorcised by a more potent witchdoctor or perhaps by religious faith. It is well known in Africa for a man to be perfectly healthy, then one day to start to ail, becoming no more than a shadow of himself, until he turns his face to the wall and dies as if he himself had willed it. Nothing can deflect the course of this condition for the patient is embroiled by a growing sense of guilt, fear and evil, often cultivated by sorcerers with weird spells and rituals. Ritual murders to provide the materials for these spells still take place in secret.

An alternative to the casting of spells is the bizarre cult of the Lion Men of Singida in central Tanzania, who might be described as trained assassins. If someone wishes to remove an enemy from the community he can hire a Lion Man from the sorcerer-owner, who will arrange the assassination. The sorcerer will have captured or bought a mentally deficient child and kept him in confinement until he is grown. Kept in his narrow space the captive can never stand upright, his nails grow to be claws, and finally he is let loose, clad in a lion's skin to act as a hired killer and terrorize the local population. A priest in Tanzania described seeing one of these sub-human apparitions. He was crouching in a pit like an animal. He spoke no language and could only grunt. Even in captivity and without his disguise he was a horrifying sight, made more terrible by being so crude a distortion of humanity. Little is known of these many cults, the most evil of which is said to come from the island of Pemba off the Tanzanian coast. The very secretiveness of the spirit cult enhances the fear in which people hold it and thereby adds to its power.

One particularly powerful witchdoctor, Kajiwe, originates from Ukambani, east of Nairobi. Forbidden by the government to return there, he now lives on the coast at Kilifi. On the principle of 'set a thief to catch a thief', he has been hired by

*A healer stands in an ancestral cave near the Kenya coast. Bathed in a shaft of light, falling from a hole in the roof of the cave, he calls upon the spirits of his ancestors. This is the Old Africa which still exists to this day, permeating many levels of African society.*

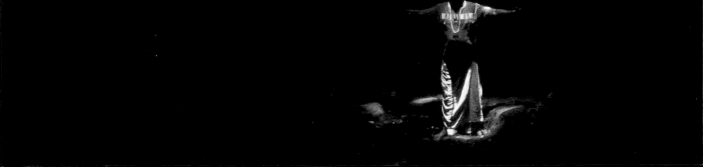

the government to stamp out witchcraft in its most evil form. Small and stocky, with a charisma about his person which centres in his powerful mesmeric eyes, he roars up and down the countryside, smelling out witches. He will often start a witch hunt late at night. The night becomes horrid with the howls and shouts of the people who follow him in droves. Among the crowd are his forty wives who accompany him everywhere while tagging along behind are his quantities of children.

My daughter Katrina witnessed one of his exorcisms. The crowd, beating drums and singing, converged on a hamlet. Kajiwe danced around shouting and brandishing a flaming torch. He dug frantically in the earth under a tree, and, sure enough, there were the telltale bones and other charms hidden by a real witch. He shouted and leapt in the air in triumph and the offending old man was handcuffed by police, made to kneel while Kajiwe urinated over him, brandishing his firebrand as part of the exorcism ceremony. The Middle Ages suddenly seemed very close, as the old witch was led away into the night. Happily in 1985 he did not face the stake, but a small fine or a few weeks in prison. Modern life has some advantages.

Innumerable diseases in Africa are said to be caused by personal enmity. It is no doubt a reflection of the deeply felt African attitude that things do not happen of themselves, but from causes beyond one's control. No one is sick from drinking dirty water, but from the ill will of an enemy, or the malice of some spirit. This attitude may be one of the biggest factors working against the progress of Africa, for until an individual accepts responsibility for himself and his family, for his deeds and their aftermath, it is difficult to enter into modern life as we know it.

There are a growing number of traditional healers who recognize modern science as a powerful source of healing and they will refer patients to doctors when they know they can do no more. This sometimes results in the patient reaching the doctor too late. Organized cooperation between the two systems could thus prove highly beneficial, although it would be necessary for modern doctors to recognize that a visit to the local healer is sometimes more useful than large doses of Valium. Western medicine could also benefit from a study of the use of ritual, which plays a large part in African medicine. Much of what is called magic is part of a symbolic ritual cleansing and renewing of the body and spirit of the patient, the importance of which was long ago emphasized by Jung.

It is difficult to relate these experiences to anything that Westerners know in their daily lives. We, who like scientific explanations for everything, are rightly puzzled by such phenomena. During the next few decades, however, our understanding may become clearer. As chaos can now be demonstrated by a mathematical equation and the new physics opens up the unseen, revealing waves and vibrations as a fifth dimension to us, so one day we may be able to recognize the beneficial and antagonistic waves coming from the unseen, which have long been known to more primitive man. His antennae are perhaps more sensitive to this realm of being, though it is interesting that almost all instances related to possession by spirits, are stories of evil spirits. Even good spirits appear to reprimand rather than comfort and restore. Perhaps these latter functions are a development of the great religions which so often overlay many of the old superstitions.

*In a scene reminiscent of the story of the Fisherman and the Genie in* Arabian Nights, *a coastal healer listens to the voice of a spirit (Jini/Genie) speaking to him from the gourd. He has removed the stopper and is holding it in his left hand.*

Superstitious belief is used as the basis for much healing and with this comes a certain accompanying fear. Whether the medicine be African or modern, we all know the fear we have of hospitals, doctors, nurses, and the instruments they use. Examinations, injections, operations, cures worse than the disease – these, and the impersonal buildings people are kept in, all produce fear rather than confidence in the healer. To be effective the healer has to overcome this innate fear. The African healer perhaps does this by invoking the impartial spirits, the ancestors who can be expected to be benevolent to their offspring. In modern hospitals patients have largely to rely on their own spiritual resources, or the painkillers and the Valium pill.

Despite the wonders western medical science has achieved for the human race, our approach to health still has grave shortcomings. While spending millions on technical advances which can benefit only the few, general conditions of treatment, which mean so much to both staff and patients, have been allowed to run down. Cuts are being enforced everywhere, where a coat of paint, new uniforms, and attention to detail could raise the morale of the service immeasurably. Priorities are difficult to decide, but where technology is beyond the budget, it should be reduced, or in some way centralized, in order to release funds for the benefit of a wider majority of patients.

Among local doctors also, modern medicine is in dire straits. The load of patients is often so great that very little personal attention is possible. No longer does the family doctor visit homes, where so much useful knowledge of the patients' background was accumulated in the past. It is easy to understand why this has happened. A doctor's consulting room, with his instruments, drugs and proper lighting, is a better place to see most patients than in their own home where these things are lacking. Most people also can avail themselves of a car or public transport to come to him, so that even their need is not the same.

Small wonder, then, that alternative medicine has expanded into many different fields – acupuncture, chiropractice, homeopathy, reflexology, to mention a few – where the patient is treated as a whole person rather than as part of an impersonal system. This approach to treatment has become the concern of many who are interested in medicine, and through new emphasis of this kind much may be gained in the knowledge of healing.

It is even more understandable in Africa, where hospitals are forbidding and alien and science is for most people a closed book, that the majority still resort to the familiar personal contact of their traditional healers. Many people play safe and use both systems, and the healers themselves play safe by using symbols from the two great religions of Africa – Christianity and Islam.

Research projects are being undertaken by the African Medical and Research Foundation (AMREF) and other organizations into many aspects of traditional medicine. Already it has been established that many of the herbs used by African herbalists contain chemicals that are used by doctors all over the world. AMREF has a whole department devoted to studying health behaviour and from this, information is building up concerning the procedures of the traditional medicine

*This Luo healer has his 'practice' near the shores of Lake Victoria. He is seen here divining a patient's problem by studying the lie of the cowrie shells in his hand.*

*This sketch is an illustration of the bizarre cult of the lion-men of Singida, a cult that has terrorized parts of central Tanzania for many years. Typically victims are found with fearful lacerations from lion claws. The local name for a Lion Man is 'Mboju'. In the late 1960s a Tanzanian policeman wrote a book in Swahili by this title, describing some of the 'assassinations' that had occurred during his period of duty.*

men, and of the needs of an African rural community in the way of personal health, care and education. These and many more fields of research are increasing our knowledge and, as more is known, it will become easier to use and assimilate these ancient medical skills into the present-day system, which so often lacks roots in social and individual experience.

As physical science advances it is seen more and more to be integrated with what is known of psychology. As a result healers of all kinds are gaining new respect in the western world. The laying on of hands, for example, though the reasons for its success are not fully understood or appreciated, is acknowledged as holding some strange power – akin indeed to that of healers in Africa, like Mwalimu in Mombasa, who also have this power. The realm of the mind, its energy, its projections, its hidden capacities will undoubtedly influence all types of medical care in the future and new depths of healing will result.

The concept of health is becoming more important than curing disease. Maybe jogging, aerobic exercises, the multitude of modern diets are our way of expressing age-old superstitions no more or less effective than the laying on of hands, the drawing out of the spirits' heat and the sprinkling of a little holy rosewater in Africa.

Recently I was flying with some friends in a helicopter, out over the bleak stretches of the Rift Valley south of Nairobi. We circled the craggy peak of Shomboli Mountain looking for ten feet of flat land on which to put down. Ridge after ridge fell abruptly into the floor of the Rift, causing us to balance shakily on the tussock grass. The expanse on either side is filled with two soda lakes, Magadi in Kenya and Natron in Tanzania. The twin lakes were in sharp contrast, for sheets of white soda covered Magadi, while a curious layer of algae made Lake Natron look as if it had been left over from a time when the earth was molten lava and fire. The one was sparkling white with black holes where the soda had melted, and the other was dark blood red, with a filigree of green and white channels criss-crossing it. Poised on the sentinel mountain in between, in a moonscape which began to lose colour as the sun lowered in the gigantic stretch of sky, we took in the contrasts of the landscape.

Our little group fell silent, our conversation hushed into awe, aware that we were present as perhaps no one had been before in a landscape oblivious of man, made out of the harsh contrasts of rock, water and sky. These contrasts, interwoven into a harmony, seemed to me to picture the many realities which live side by side in Africa. They produce a pattern of exquisite variety. We need now only to become aware of its riches.

*Extracts from local African advertisements of the 1950s for traditional potions.*

# CHAPTER TWO

# THE CROCODILE EATERS

...............................................

It was Monday morning, and already I was working at a desk piled high with letters to be answered and files to be dealt with. It was a morning of crystal clear views after rain, and big clouds sailed over the little civil airport where Flying Doctors had their office and hangar. As I put my signature to the last of a pile of letters the telephone rang, and a voice came up from the Radio Room.

'Mr Wood, can you come down and speak to the police from Lokichoggio? They have had a bad raid in the night and many people have been killed.'

'I'll come right down,' I said, and leaving my pen where it lay and the letter unfolded, I went over quickly to the Radio Room.

The report from the police was as bad as I feared. It was once again a border raid into Turkana territory from the southern Sudan and there were a few survivors in need of urgent medical help.

'I'll be with you in three hours,' I said into the radio, and immediately set about packing our emergency kit into the Cherokee which was one of two aeroplanes that Flying Doctors had at that time.

The flight from Nairobi to Turkana is one of the most interesting in East Africa. It shows so clearly, in the pattern of the mountains, forests and deserts, what is happening along Africa's rugged contours, a sight which can only really be appreciated from the air – the great distances become the dimension of the flyer, and the marks of time and tempest can be traced. On this particular morning as the sun rose, I saw as never before the green and fertile land of the Kenya Highlands, productive and teeming with population, set like an island in the surrounding desert, for as you drop over the edge of the Rift Valley escarpment you enter a different world. The country is dry and inhospitable and the further north you go the drier it becomes.

The Turkana region is like its name, cruel and harsh, but has a grandeur of primeval proportions. The people who live there have become like the country, having developed a workable harmony with their tough surroundings. Survival is the main occupation. It demands all of man's strength and ingenuity and most of his time. The Turkana live under a relentless sun and have become inured to its effects. They are tall with colourful headdresses and bead adornments; their faces are heavy-featured, reminding one of the rocks among which they live.

The region borders what is sometimes known as the Jade Sea, formerly Lake Rudolf, but now called Lake Turkana – a great sheet of water stretching 180 miles north and south along the Great Rift Valley. The shores of the lake are mostly desert with occasional groups of ragged palm trees, stripped to ribbons by the gale, which blows day and night for most of the year. On the western shore two seasonal rivers, the Turkwell and the Kerio, feed the lake from deltas which spread out like the fingers of a hand. Through swamps, like lurid green oases in this land of rock and sand, these rivers pour their muddy contents into the lake so that their flow can be seen right out in the centre of the lake. One can imagine the erosion which has taken place in their upper reaches. To the south the lake is guarded by an area of black lava boulders which are terrible to walk across, and which lead up to the crater summit of Mount Teleki, named after a famous Hungarian explorer who reached this land in the 1880s. High cliffs complete the coastline of these treacherous waters, which lap persistently on the rocky shore. The waters are famous for their blue-green colour, but there are times when storms blow up without warning, and the surface of the lake is whipped up into waves. These squalls have been known to drown many a boatman, which is why the Turkana have never taken to boats and do not eat fish.

The bulk of the Turkana region lies to the west of the lake. Twenty miles from the shore, a small town called Lodwar crouches uneasily at the foot of a dark conical mountain, Lodwar Mountain, which is a local landmark. Lodwar is the provincial capital of Turkana. Dust whips round the mission buildings and hospital, swirling down the mainstreet, where small shops and hovels cluster round a ramshackle beer shop. Lodwar does not boast many comforts and the prevailing elements seem to be the desert dust and the wind.

This desert stretches through Turkana to the Sudan border, across the Sudan into Chad, and across Niger, Mali and Mauritania to the Atlantic itself. There are only a few isolated areas of fertility in the desert, which is encroaching southwards year by year. It is an awesome menace, more dangerous than the hostile neighbours

...........................................

*(Opposite) Like the Maasai, the Turkana are blood drinkers and, according to Joy Adamson, the only people in Africa whose diet includes lion and crocodile. This Turkana warrior has a clay bun into which decorative feathers can be fixed.*

...........................................

*(Previous page) The sun goes down over Lake Turkana with South Island silhouetted in the foreground. Lying in the deserts of the Great Rift Valley, this lake is nearly 200 miles long. In 1934 an English doctor and an American surveyor set out for South Island in a small boat. For several nights their camp fires were observed from the mainland but then disappeared and the two men never returned. A subsequent search using camels, aircraft and a boat revealed no trace of them or their vessel. It is thought that they were either attacked by crocodiles or sank in a squall.*

38

whom countries spend so much time trying to combat.

Several hours' flying brought me and the nurse I had taken with me to the small airstrip of Lokichoggio which in the flat desert hardly showed at all, a mere light shadow in the grey landscape. We landed, scattering dust and stones in all directions. The police officer in charge came out to meet the aeroplane and took us hurriedly to the village which had been attacked.

I shall never forget the scene of devastation which greeted us. All the cattle and goats had been driven off and the ground was strewn with human bodies. The village dogs were already at their gruesome task of cleaning up. They sniffed around the corpses and some had even begun to eat them. Here and there a leg or an arm lay like a fruit broken open, giving a ghastly touch to the scene. At our appearance the dogs growled menacingly and slunk off to another corpse, regarding us with an evil eye. It is a grisly thought that these animals could return to devour their former masters and, although they are the sanitation system of the desert, this habit spreads disease and has become the curse of the area.

We searched among the dead for signs of life. Rounding a burnt hut, I came upon two children pinned to the ground with spears and still alive. They were gasping with shock and thirst, and pain had almost stifled consciousness. Slowly, and with infinite care, we sawed off the top-heavy spears. They were so shocked that bleeding was minimal. We gently loaded the pathetic survivors into the plane and abandoned the carnage to the cleansers of the desert, dogs, jackals, hyenas and vultures which already filled the air.

We flew south to the hospital at Lodwar and operated on the two children. The first, a little girl, had been fairly fortunate and the spear had not penetrated any vital organ. We managed to extract the blade and repair the damage and she lived. The young boy was not so lucky, for when we extracted the blade, a huge haemorrhage flooded the operating table and his life, which was hanging by a thread, quietly left him.

This incident was in what now seems the dim past, when the Flying Doctor Service only had two aeroplanes and had its offices in a go-down for the airport for a rent of £7 a month. The small wars in the north, the cattle raids which swung back and forth over the frontiers, were all fought with spears and huge knives called simis. It was a more intimate and personal way of fighting but no kinder than the gun which has to a great extent superseded cold steel. The rip of a bullet from a distance, with no personal struggle involved, is equally deadly, and the introduction of automatic weapons is of course infinitely more devastating. In fact the proliferation of modern automatic weapons has become a serious problem in this

............................................

*(Opposite) Until recently cattle raiding was done with sticks and spears, but the escalation of armed conflicts in the neighbouring territories of Uganda, Sudan and Ethiopia has led to an influx of weapons and ammunition. Now cattle raiding is a more serious business and hundreds may die in a big raid.*

............................................

*(Previous page) Children walk through a grove of palms at Loyangalani Oasis in the cool of an early morning. Loyangalani lies on the south-east shore of Lake Turkana at a point where springs of hot, clear water gush from the lava boulders.*

*A Turkana man's chair and pillow is his head rest which he carries with him at all times. Apart from a 'rungu' (stick) this is usually all he carries on his travels.*

part of Africa. Guns have been smuggled in from neighbouring Ethiopia and Uganda. Amin's disbanded army and the Sudanese, Ethiopian and Somalian wars have all contributed towards the growing arsenals. Police stations and army barracks have been raided, and looted weapons add to the chaos, replacing the old spears, rungus and simis. Lawlessness is on the increase and the man with the gun calls the tune. Those with ammunition are often even more influential than those with guns, as the former is often in short supply.

Operating in local hospitals with very restricted facilities obviously presents problems, but even when it is possible to take patients to the larger centres where more sophisticated facilities are available, other difficulties can arise. The shock which people like the Turkana experience, when flown from a remote settlement like Lokichoggio to a big hospital in Nairobi, can easily be imagined. From their homes in the desert, their nights spent under the stars, they find themselves surrounded by strangers in a huge building, the like of which they have never seen before. Often they are housed several storeys up with no view of the ground and no one about who can speak their language. This was one of the main reasons why we started the flying surgical service which carries surgeons out to the bush hospitals rather than bringing patients into the centres. In bush hospitals they have their families near them and remain in their own surroundings, in a familiar atmosphere which they can understand. Anyone who has spent a night in the open, under the roof of African stars, will understand the terrible claustrophobia which can overwhelm the spirit of the nomad confined in a hospital ward.

As the years went by we had increasing evidence of the incidence of hydatid disease in the Turkana district and so we started a small research project at Lodwar to investigate the disease. This is one of the most serious diseases that the Turkana have had to face and has reached epidemic proportions, seen nowhere else in the

44

world. It was this factor in particular that prompted AMREF to select Turkana as the obvious place to conduct the project. Initially it was based at Lodwar but recently the site was moved to Lokichoggio, the scene of the tribal raid.

Hydatid disease comes from a parasite, a type of tapeworm which lives in the intestine and produces cysts in the human body. These cysts can occur anywhere, but particularly affect the lungs, abdomen, liver or bone. They can attain enormous size and weight, and debilitate the host until starvation sets in. So far the huge tumours have been dealt with surgically, with the attendant risk of spilling some of the tiny cysts in the body to grow again.

The research team at Lokichoggio are now investigating animal hosts such as dogs, camels, cattle and goats. They have built a series of neat log cabins for staff houses and laboratories. Built up in its formative years by Dr Marcus French, who did much to make the intrusion of the research acceptable to the Turkana, the project has since been taken over by a young Scotsman, Calum MacPherson, who with his vivacious young wife Caroline now heads the research station. At times one is tempted to feel that a station so remote could become lonely, especially for the young. But thanks to air communications and radio, there is nowhere in Kenya that is completely out of touch, and the further one is in the bush the more easily visitors seem to reach one. And, of course, such visitors do not drop in for tea, but stay for several days and nights at a time. So Calum and Caroline MacPherson live a busy life in this remote spot.

A biologist, Calum MacPherson came to work for AMREF in 1983. He was undaunted by the remote area in which he was required to live for he was already deeply interested in the problem of hydatid disease which he was about to tackle. Through this work, which is associated with many veterinary problems, he met and married Caroline who is a trained veterinarian and uncommonly pretty into the bargain. She is a fair-haired English beauty which is a constant surprise in those harsh surroundings. The two of them work closely together on the research programme although the recent arrival of a small MacPherson may interfere with this routine.

The tiny village of Lokichoggio comprises a police station and a few cor-rugated iron shacks, housing shops which sell sugar, salt, matches and other basic commodities. This is the only source of supplies for the MacPhersons and their research station, apart from what they bring from Nairobi. Lokichoggio is the furthest corner of Kenya, two and a half days' journey by road from Nairobi in dry weather. It is situated in the Elemi triangle which for many decades has been famous for the feuds raging back and forth over the three frontiers of Kenya, Ethiopia and the Sudan which meet there. Under the British it was agreed that the Kenya service would police it, and this custom still holds, although it has become a no man's land. It is a frontier post surrounded on all sides by desert for hundreds of miles.

The MacPhersons in their wooden house have up to five other research staff billeted on them. Sometimes one or two are out on safari, but it is a communal life, which can become crowded when visitors arrive. Perhaps the spaces of the desert help both the married couple and the staff to keep an equilibrium in such circumstances. Fresh supplies are brought in by air by AMREF planes passing on their way to Juba.

For the Turkana who live alongside the MacPhersons life is precarious. Survival, which is their main concern, is so tenuous that the merest shift in population could upset the whole balance of life in the area. It is difficult to imagine the life they lead under the blazing sun, washed by gigantic storms which grow to phenomenal intensity in the floor of the Rift Valley in which Lake Turkana lies. When in 1977 immense rain storms poured some seventy inches of rain onto this hard ground, white flowers appeared everywhere, and for some people they were the first flowers that they had ever seen. The small amount of top soil which had accumulated in fissures in the ground was washed away, and the desert was the same again, apart from fresh runnels of erosion down every crack and valley.

The Turkana live with immense distances. The great desert spaces seem totally empty and yet if one stops to mend a puncture, someone will appear out of nowhere, as if by magic. It is a landscape which has been untouched by man in all these centuries of life on earth. Time does not intrude into their lives at all. Heat, thirst, food and survival and the next cattle raid are the measurements by which they calculate distance and time. Change is almost unheard of, which again diminishes the sense of time.

Despite these sometimes cruel, and always harsh conditions, the human family retains its ancient pattern and strength. Families exist and are held together within the tribe, and the tribe exists to protect those families against the enemies that menace their desert life. Family love is probably not expressed in words, as is our practice, but in the solidarity with which the unit meets the struggle of life. Joy, too, is there, laughter and play, and when disaster hits, the reaction of the desert man is found in the enigma of silence, the total silence of the desert itself.

The Turkana have evolved a way of sleeping on the rocky surface of their world. They fashion a piece of wood, curved to the shape of the neck, and lying flat on their backs support their heads on this small wooden rest, which they can carry with them and use also to sit on. They wear wrist knives, a sharp piece of metal fitting round the wrist with a blade about two inches wide, sharp and circular, which can produce horrible wounds in a fight. These belongings, together with a spear, simi, and a bunch of sticks for controlling their cattle, are probably the sum of a Turkana man's possessions. The pots and pans and family goods do not hamper his march through the desert; these are carried by camels and are the affair of the women and children.

The Turkana are dependent on their cattle for food, and the survival of the cattle is sometimes even more vital for the family or tribe as a whole than the survival of a child. Thus the water for their cattle is the basic and overwhelming need in the life of the Turkana.

By far the most serious problem with which the research staff at Lockichoggio have to live is this scarcity of water. There is a borehole which serves the three villages and the surrounding area in which some 12,000 people live, plus their cattle, camels and goats. During the rains there are mudholes and the sand rivers fill with water, relieving the pressure on the borehole. In the long drawn-out dry season, however, as the heat mounts and surface water dries up, more and more cattle come in to be watered at the borehole. There are queues right through the night. Fights can break out and newcomers are not welcome.

During the time when David and I stayed there last year a fight erupted between the Turkana and the project staff. Despite the fact that the borehole was built by AMREF and the water supply was only there thanks to them, the Turkana did not recognize the staff's need for water. The little research station thus finds it difficult to gain access and carry away the few buckets a day which are needed. The Turkana, although they respect the need of cattle for water, have long ago found other means for humans to do without water almost completely. It is difficult therefore for them to understand the need of non-Turkana people for water. As a substitute for water the Turkana use their dogs for all sanitary purposes. Dogs clean up the children after they have been sick or defecated, and eat the human faeces around the village and any offal left lying around. They even eat human corpses or dead animals, if they are not buried, and burial can be a problem in the hard rocky ground. The dogs keep the inhabited area of the desert clean, but they are the source of hydatid disease and the reason why it has reached epidemic proportions. The dogs eat the remains of an infected goat and then with their muzzles covered with worm eggs, they will lick out the cooking pots of the family or tidy up after a baby with diarrhoea. Very soon the entire family is infected and the cycle begins again. An infected dog produces 40 million eggs a week, so the problem is sizeable.

The research team have started a control programme and are aiming to dose and render immune all the dogs in the area. By shooting some, and keeping the remaining population in reasonable proportions, they can dose them every six weeks, thus preventing a recurrence of the disease. Humans are treated with the new drug Albendazol which is so far proving very successful in reducing internal cysts until they are finally absorbed.

The rest of the programme is concerned with educating the population. Songs, plays, talks and all manner of entertainment are used to obtain the cooperation, firstly of the women, who are more receptive than the men. 'Don't feed dogs cysts' is the slogan, and the message is beginning to gain ground. One man, who had to go on a long journey, came to the research station to take his dog's dose with him, so that he would not miss it. Such incidents are encouraging, but the total problem will take years to control and even Australia and New Zealand have failed to eradicate the disease entirely.

Round about the research station are some local Turkanas who are employed to look after the kennels and to act as watchmen and water carriers. Their tall figures lope idly about the compound with a singular arrogance and an independence which is the outstanding characteristic of their tribe. In the first few months that they were working for the MacPhersons they would suddenly be irritatingly absent. No explanation could be found, until Calum realized that his headman was also leader of the local cattle raiders and, if some cattle were stolen, he had immediately to organize reprisals or even initiate an adventure or two of his own. Now that the situation is understood, he and his followers will come and ask permission to leave, and it is tacitly understood that he suddenly has more important work to do.

Cattle raiding is a tribal tradition. A Turkana man cannot receive the honour of tattoo scars on his chest or back until he has killed five men. A tattoo on the shoulders represents only two or three dead men. These warriors whose staple diet is milk and blood do not recognize territorial boundaries. They slip as easily into Ethiopia or the Sudan as they go raiding their Pokot neighbours. Everyone in the north talks of 'going down to Kenya', which to them is another country. To them Turkana is its own country, with familiar migration routes followed every year to the distant grazing areas. Gifted with an acute sense of observation, they can spot edible berries and find edible roots in the bleakest terrain. A Turkana can walk fifty miles a night in his long rhythmic strides, often barefoot or else in crude sandals made from motor car tyres. Every herder nowadays will carry a gun or stolen automatic weapon, such as have found their way into the hands of raiders on all sides in the north.

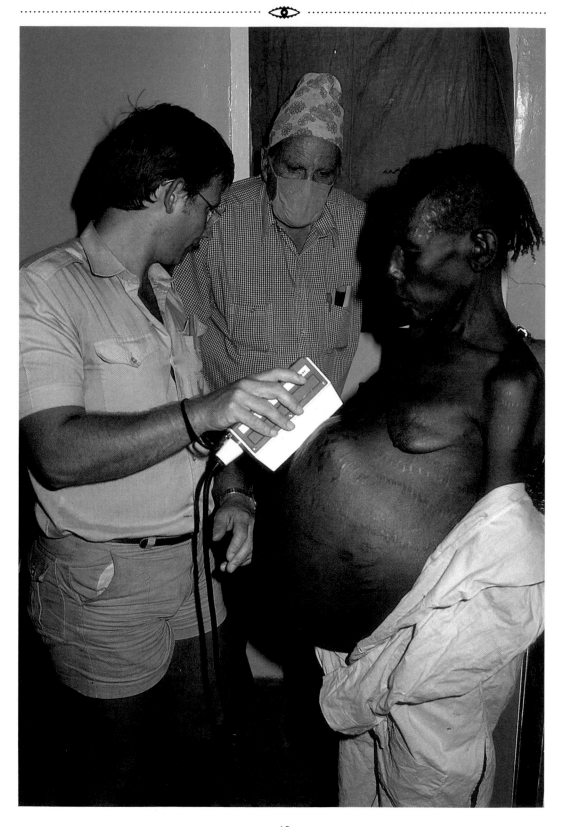

*Crocodiles breed in the volcanic lakes of Central Island, Lake Turkana.*

..................................................

*(Opposite) A woman patient with large abdominal hydatid cysts being scanned using ultrasound equipment, prior to operation. This disease comes from a parasite, a type of tapeworm which is carried by dogs and passed on to children and adults.*

..................................................

Men are still the dominant faction in Turkana life. As with all these northern warrior tribes, the women are kept in total subservience. Calum and Caroline, at the time of their marriage, gave a great wedding feast for the whole village. The women arrived in the early afternoon and danced till sunset, when the great roasts of meat were ready. The men swept in and ate every bit and the women were sent home hungry and embittered. The MacPhersons then gave a party especially for the women to make up for the unhappy ending of the previous affair. It was not customary, however, for the women to eat, except in their own homes. So after some celebration they took their meat and returned happily homewards.

One of the initial drawbacks in controlling hydatid disease resulted from the tribe's fondness for beads. People who had the disease for the first time were given a bright red bead to wear, with a number on it for easy identification; the beads also indicated that the wearer was being treated with Albendazol. However, brightly coloured beads are in great demand as part of the traditional garb of Turkana men and women, and it was no time before our beads were being sold or traded in for goats and other commodities.

But this is not the only frustration that Calum and his staff have had to contend with. Since my visit with David last year, Lokichoggio has again been raided, this time by the Toposa tribe, and some of his staff were killed. The other day he called on a woman to talk about the inoculation of her dogs. She gave him a withering look, saying, 'My husband has been killed, my son and daughter are dead, and you come and talk to me about worms in my dogs? Get out of here!' Suddenly compared

49

to the raid, the ravages of hydatid seemed trivial and unimportant.

Hydatid is not the only parasite disease that occurs in this region. Kala-azar is another unpleasant disease which takes a heavy toll. Passed on from the bite of a sand fly, it is characterized by prolonged fever, leading to wasting of the body and enlargement of the spleen and liver. As a result of a reduction in their white blood corpuscles, victims become very anaemic. Its symptoms are not unlike those of malaria, which causes problems in diagnosis since the two can be easily confused. It can, however, be treated with antimony compounds, although three courses of treatment are often required before the parasite is finally eradicated.

One of the long-term side effects of research into, and control of, hydatid and other diseases will be to enable meat from these huge cattle areas in the Third World to be sold on the world market, whereas it is at present condemned. This could be a significant source of wealth to these areas. Yet when one talks of wealth, in the Western sense, one begins to be afraid for these people. Living so precariously in the inhospitable desert, can wealth in the Western sense do anything for them but alter their way of life so drastically that they will cease to exist in their time-honoured system and age-old environment?

People have often advocated, or assumed, that nomadic life should gradually be replaced by settled populations and the development of an agricultural community. Those who know the desert and have come to respect its peoples and their way of life, would contest this view. Any interference with the ecology of such areas would almost certainly mean the extinction of its peoples. Perhaps the more adaptable of its young might survive to live a different life in other surroundings; but the land itself, so fragile in its balance, producing barely enough grass and scrub for the small population, would rapidly become like the Sahara, devoid of life altogether. Dramatic inroads by Western medicine, a sudden increase in the population, all could spell disaster to both the people and the area. Here we need the respect for life as Albert Schweitzer advocated – an understanding reticence, a readiness to help in disaster, but above all the timeless patience of the desert.

Such reflections however, may already be too late, for a new tarmac road has already reached Lodwar and is destined to be completed one day as far as Juba. This means that heavy traffic will pass through Turkana bound for the southern Sudan and beyond. It will inevitably intrude into the traditional life of the people. As oil has now been found in the Sudan, a far greater intrusion may take place in the form of a possible pipeline, and the people to run such an enterprise will bring new demands and new ideas.

At the same time Turkana will become accessible, and we can only hope that this will bring in its train benefits and not disaster for the Turkana people. Only nomadic people seem to have learnt the art of living in the desert, and those who would alter their circumstances should bear in mind that big schemes seldom work. Development is dependent on being able to change the thinking of the people themselves. If you fail in this, then the project will be a flash in the pan, and will not survive your departure. Like a sand river in flood it will be impressive while the

*(Opposite above) The Turkana are never happier than when they are dancing. Like the Maasai, the warriors specialize in jumping high off the ground.*

*(Opposite below) The AMREF laboratory at Lokichoggio near the Kenya/ Sudan border where the hydatid research programme is carried out. Hydatid disease has reached epidemic proportions in this region of Kenya.*

water lasts, then it will revert to being exactly the same sand river that it has been since time immemorial, except for a little more debris clogging the banks.

On the return journey from Turkana, I sometimes deliberately stray a little to the east to fly down the lake. Often I try to imagine what it was like when my father-in-law, Alfred Buxton, who was working there as a missionary, walked round it in the early 1930s. Old photographs of him in his tent show him writing his diary. There were no modern comforts then, just loneliness and the waves lapping on the desert shore. From the aircraft I see the volcanic islands strung down the centre of the lake as much as fifty miles apart. The first one is North Island followed soon by Central Island with its emerald-coloured crater lakes infested with crocodiles. Finally, at the south end, South Island comes into view.

South Island is uninhabited, but boasts a herd of strange wild goats. These were first discovered by Fuchs in 1934 during the Lake Rudolf expedition of which he was leader. According to Turkana legend the island, which lies fifteen miles offshore, was once inhabited and connected with the mainland. One day, however, the linking spit of land sank beneath the waves, marooning the Turkanas and their goats on what is now the island. For some months, says the legend, their fires could be seen at night, but when these went out those on the mainland knew that they had died, although the goats survived as goats usually do. Geological evidence supports the possibility that the legend records an actual historical event which occurred a thousand or more years ago. The story has been accurately handed down over the generations and illustrates the strength of the oral tradition in societies like this. Sadly, Fuchs' expedition ended in disaster, for after he had returned to the mainland, two of his men sailed over to the island and were never seen again. He believes that their boat must have sunk in a gale and that they were drowned or eaten by crocodiles.

As I fly my view to the east is uninterrupted for 300 miles, until the Chalbi desert flows into the Marsabit Mountain, which juts abruptly from its floor. Another 200 miles to the east and the white flat-roofed houses of Wajir shimmer in the heat. There is nothing in between to serve as a landmark or guideline.

I fly on with an increasing sense of wonder. I am encapsulated in my cockpit surrounded by the miracles of modern technology, yet I look out at the lake and the desert – a rugged, primeval world. The contrast between this timelessness and the calculations I make for fuel, altitude and distance is almost too great to assimilate. Soon I will be having supper in my Nairobi home, but down there the animals are being herded into thorn enclosures to protect them from marauding lions.

Night comes swiftly in the desert and with its arrival the day ends abruptly. For the Turkana gathered round a small fire, if they have been lucky enough to come across some sticks for firewood, activity ceases with the arrival of the dark. They live off camel's milk, goat's milk and sometimes blood, and so no cooking fills the early hours of the night. There is no water available for washing and when talk is exhausted there is nothing to do but sleep. An animal becomes restless in the night, and the men of the family rouse and watch for intruders, two-legged or otherwise. A comfortless and dangerous existence and yet it is lived amid the extraordinary peace of the earth itself beneath the expanses of the wide sky.

*The most comfortable way of carrying a Nile Perch is on your head. This Turkana girl near Molo Bay is wearing a long beaded skirt which indicates that she has reached puberty.*

# CHAPTER THREE

# HEROINES OF THE DESERT

..............................................

It was a bright December morning when David and I set off to fly to Wajir, another desert area in the north of Kenya. We were fully loaded for a long operating session. My African theatre sister kept a possessive eye on our instrument boxes as they were loaded, and David studied the maps for the long flight ahead.

Once airborne we saw Mount Kilimanjaro, its snowy summit glittering a hundred miles to the south, and Mount Kenya, the same distance to the north, stabbing its sharp pinnacles into a hot brassy sky. The Aberdare range rolled away to the west as we skirted over the multitude of ridges that run down the eastern side of Mount Kenya. We flew over the Tana River at the Great Cataract, and then headed out over the huge expanse of country to the north. Land and sky blurred into one, and I leant forward in the cockpit searching for the pencil-line of road which I knew would lead us across this lonely terrain to the isolated town of Wajir. Navigation in this area is difficult since the radio beacon in Wajir has not been working for many months, and there can be very strong winds in the north which blow you far off course.

The flight from Nairobi takes two hours and I began to check my watch, hoping we had not missed Wajir and were not now headed for Ethiopia. Suddenly with relief in his voice, David pointed out the track of road below us, and we dropped a few hundred feet, the better to follow it. We clung to this slender thread, as it wandered through the Lorian swamp and on across the desert, until a tiny fringe of white buildings, quivering in the heat as if seen through water, became visible in the blur ahead.

Wajir lies in the remote north-eastern corner of Kenya. It is a dusty little town some 500 miles from any other town of size, in the middle of a desert area which, in heavy rain, reverts to swamp. Bristling thorn bushes grow out of the grey sand for miles in every direction. Anyone so ill-advised as to leave the road can get hopelessly lost within minutes, so flat and monotonous, so spotted with thorn bush, is the landscape. There is no surface water for hundreds of miles in any direction though Wajir itself is famous for its wells. Legend has it that some three thousand years ago the Queen of Sheba watered her camels here. Today the scene could easily be the same, as thousands of camels stand in orderly groups round the wells, waiting to be watered.

The wells are only about twenty feet deep and are undoubtedly of great antiquity. Old skin buckets are let down and raised in a rhythmic motion, the water splashing amid cries, singing, the grunts of camels and the bleating of goats. The buckets are emptied in a circular trough surrounding the well head and the camels drink soberly, patiently, after their long weeks of browsing through the barren country.

The white buildings of the town with little minarets rising above tessellated houses have the atmosphere of a Foreign Legion fort. Wajir is an administrative centre, with a district commissioner, police, hospital and army camp. On the wall behind the DC's desk are recorded the illustrious names of former DCs of the colonial era, now passed into history. On the outskirts of the town a strange-shaped building, named by some humorist in the colonial service 'The Wajir Yacht Club', used to be a meeting place for officers of all services. The streets of soft dust have few vehicles to scatter the small children playing on the ground and a few white-washed stones, arranged in a circle, act as a traffic roundabout at one end of the main thoroughfare. There are two or three grocer's shops, a butcher's, a maker of sweet cakes, a cemetery hidden behind a low stone wall, overgrown by weeds, and then the desert, containing and dominating everything. A timeless quality seems to pervade the whole atmosphere. On this particular morning, as David and I flew in on our medical mission, the flat arid land looked, from the air, like the floor of an ancient lake, an old sea bed from the far-off geological past.

This oasis in the north east of Kenya is inhabited largely by Somalis. These lean Moslem tribesmen are nomads, living with their camels in symbiotic fashion. The camel walks to its grazing, accompanied by its owner and his family, and only needs to return to the wells after three weeks' absence. The family survives on the camel's milk, while the camels carry the few possessions of the family, who walk alongside them. They are the only domesticated animals designed to survive without water in these pitiless wastelands. Their huge spongy feet are adapted to walking on the soft sand, but it is their ability to survive without water and still give milk that makes them not only indispensable but the basis of human life in the desert.

The freedom of this life lies deep in the heart of these nomads. They defend it fanatically and are only happy in their natural environment. They are fierce and cruel, and indulge in fighting among their clans and with their neighbours, particularly the Ethiopians. In the past, as their grazing areas became exhausted they would raid southwards, extending their territory. The colonial era put a stop to this, but since Kenya's independence they have tried politically, and through poaching and banditry, to annexe the north-eastern part of Kenya. These days they are often armed with modern automatic weapons captured from raids over the border. Life is

*(Opposite) Flying over Kenya's north-eastern province you can see Africa stretching away in every direction. The town here is Wajir where, legend has it, the Queen of Sheba watered her camels nearly 3000 years ago.*

*(Previous page) Fresh water gushes from the rocks at Kalacha Goda, one of the Chalbi Desert's most beautiful oases. Every day thousands of camels come to drink here and the women fill their bottles for the next leg of their long journey.*

cheap and the will of Allah is inexorable, accepted with the fatalism that is part of their strength.

We had come to Wajir to visit a remarkable Rehabilitation Centre where a community of Italian women had gathered the cripples and outcasts of the area. I also had a list of operations to do at the government hospital. We circled the town looking down into the little hidden courtyards of the houses at the children, the day's washing strung up, and the general confusion of human living which is not visible from the streets with their high white walls.

I circled the aircraft once more for we were about to land on the huge tarmac strip used by the Kenya Air Force, and I was apprehensive that some jet fighter whose call I had not picked up on our small radio might slice in front of us. But a welcome signal was received from ground control and we came in gently to land. Feeling like a fly on a sea of tarmac we taxied off hurriedly to the shade of a thorn tree where we could comfortably unload and refuel.

We were fortunate to be able to fly up, because the journey by road can take three to five days. Vehicles have to travel in convoy owing to the presence of 'Shifta' (Somali bandits) who will otherwise attack unaccompanied vehicles. On the long stretches of sandy road it is simple for the Shifta to see vehicles coming, from the dust they throw up in their wake. An ambush is usually arranged in a dry river bed or wherever there is cover in which to hide. The vehicles are sitting ducks, and often everything is taken from them including food supplies, clothing and guns. Now convoys are arranged with escorts, and usually about twenty vehicles set out together. They go slowly, and if one vehicle breaks down they all have to stop until it is mended, a tedious and dangerous business, and an ordeal for the children and staff from the Rehabilitation Centre when they have to travel down to Nairobi.

AMREF, however, as part of its specialist services, sends doctors and nurses to Wajir by air to help with some of the medical and surgical problems, and an eye specialist makes regular routine visits. Our eldest son, Mark, is an eye surgeon who comes here regularly. On these occasions, the aircraft is always loaded to the roof with medical supplies, surgical instruments, food, spare parts, newspapers and mail. These aerial safaris are important in bringing specialist services to the most isolated areas of the country, thus improving the standard of health care available in remote districts. It also has the advantage that patients can be treated near their homes with the minimum dislocation in their lives, while urban hospitals do not become over-crowded.

The government hospital at Wajir has fortunately been improved by the addition of running water and electric light. These amenities were installed by my son, Mark, when he was stationed at Wajir for two years as Medical Officer in the early seventies. In addition AMREF has installed a high frequency radio at the hospital for calling our Nairobi headquarters, always referred to as 'Foundation Control'. These radios have made a big difference to life at isolated stations. They have given remote hospitals a feeling of security and the chance of medical back-up in emergencies when immediate contact with Nairobi is vital. Medical advice can be given over the radio about difficult cases and when necessary, an aircraft from AMREF's Flying Doctor Service can be sent to evacuate a patient quickly to a

*Striking portrait of a Gabbra woman. Like their Somali neighbours, the Gabbra always appear cool and unruffled even after walking barefoot through the lava desert in the scorching heat of the day.*

referral hospital. In the case of the children of the home, some have been operated on in Wajir, others taken to Wamba, a mission hospital some 200 miles away, and some taken all the way to Nairobi, when special laboratory tests or X-rays have been required. Radio communication makes these journeys both simple and quick to arrange.

The Rehabilitation Centre's Land Rover was there to meet us, and with the help of the Centre's staff we unloaded and reloaded the stores and instruments we had brought. Our assistants looked eagerly through the mail and scanned the newspapers for news of the outside world. The drive to the other side of this small town is not far, and we arrived outside the Centre in time to do a day's work.

Enclosed in a perimeter wall, the Centre is built round a central courtyard, off which radiate a series of rooms. On the right is a large gymnasium which has all the equipment, such as walking machines and parallel bars, necessary for physiotherapy. The staffrooms surround the courtyard and ahead is a corridor leading through the dining room and kitchens to a small guest house. Fortunately for the Centre they have their own well, so there is plenty of water, not only for themselves and their patients, but for the trees and shrubs which give a lovely shade in the courtyard. Beyond the buildings is a garden in which sufficient fruit and vegetables are grown to supply everyone at the Centre, which shows how fruitful the desert can become when near-surface water is used for irrigation.

The morning light was not yet strong and the day's heat was building up slowly. I sat in the cool shade of an oleander tree which was covered with pink flowers, as the patients gathered around. A Land Rover drew up, and out of it spilled a crowd of children of various ages. Crutches and calipers in all directions, they leapt and hobbled, laughing and teasing each other, as they made noisily for the gymnasium. Maria Asunta, one of the community's helpers, a small spry lady full of laughter, had been on her round picking up crippled children from all over town. She bustled her charges into the gymnasium and the chaos assumed order. The day's exercises began.

At that moment Annalena Tonelli came out of the kitchen to greet us – a strikingly handsome woman of forty, with an air of authority and energy about her. Some twelve years ago Annalena, a school teacher from Forli in northern Italy, was teaching at a school in Mandera, a town in the extreme north-eastern point of Kenya where Ethiopia, Somalia and Kenya join borders. Like Wajir this is a dry and arid region inhabited largely by people of Somali origin. It was in Mandera that Annalena saw the tragedy of children who had the misfortune to contract diseases such as polio or measles, with the ensuing aftermath of deformity and blindness. The terrible choice which confronts Somali parents hampered with a sick child can easily be understood: they must live with their camels and follow the grazing patterns, or perish. As in the animal world, nature is cruel: only the fittest survive,

*(Opposite) Two Somali girls in front of a large herd of camels at Wajir. Up to 5000 camels may come to drink at these ancient wells on any one day.*

*(Previous page) A Gabbra village 'on the move' in the Chalbi Desert, south of the Huri Hills. Curved hut poles and animal skins are packed on the camels' backs. Like the Somalis, the Gabbras' lives revolve round their camels.*

the rest go to the wall. Even the old people who finally cannot keep up are given a little milk or water, and abandoned in the desert for the hyenas to finish off. Living alongside these people and seeing the hardship of their lives, Annalena decided to do something to help. She started to collect the outcasts and founded a community outside Wajir where they could be cared for. She built the Rehabilitation Centre with money raised by friends and relatives in Italy. Over the years the numbers have grown and it has become a haven for the sick, disabled and destitute.

It was not long before Annalena realized that one of the greatest scourges of the area was TB. One can visualize how easy and rapid the spread of this disease would be in a nomadic community. Firstly they have no resistance to this disease for it is foreign to the continent as a whole. Added to this inbuilt susceptibility is the proximity to each other in which they live. Their houses consist of a bundle of sticks with skins thrown over them. It is possible to lie down very close together inside them but it is not possible to stand up or move around. They are like small two-man tents, very portable and light, but also conducive to the spread of disease.

Efforts to cure cases were usually abortive because patients failed to take their drugs regularly. Often when they felt better they would simply disappear again with their camels. The idea of remaining in one place for a long period for treatment was totally foreign to their nomadic way of life.

The government therefore set up a TB village next to the Centre, to isolate and treat people suffering from this disease. On the morning of our arrival Annalena proudly showed us round the village where she personally supervises the administration of the drugs, waking each morning at 3 am to make sure no one misses their regular dose. There are now 240 inmates living in simple grass houses which they build themselves. The cure rate in the village is now 96 per cent, due entirely to Annalena's vigilance in seeing that the drugs are taken regularly. The length of the treatment used to be about eighteen months, but modern drugs have enabled this period to be reduced to six months.

Among the Somalis TB can run a rapid downhill course if not treated. Like leprosy, it has earned a reputation, and patients tend to be socially ostracized because everyone knows how catching it is. Diagnosis is also complicated by the fact that sufferers will not admit to the symptoms for fear of this ostracism. However, the biggest problem in Kenya with TB is still the percentage of defaulters. As soon as they begin to feel better on the drugs, they stop taking them, and the disease returns more resistant than ever. TB can affect any part of the body, but the lungs are the most common site, followed by the lymph glands in the neck. It can also attack the bones and joints particularly the spine. If spinal TB is not treated in time paralysis will ensue and the victims will then probably be abandoned. In the Wajir village the patients have each other for company, live in comparatively spacious houses and there is no defaulting in the regular administration of the drugs.

This reminds me of a remark made by a friend that 'Perhaps our most disturbing deficiency is not the lack of knowledge, but our inability to use the knowledge we have.' This statement is reinforced by the statistic that 80 per cent of diseases in Africa are preventable or curable. The communicable diseases form the bulk of these, and are usually curable if the patient reports in time, and the appropriate medicines are available; and if, as Annalena might add, 'they take the drugs regularly'.

Annalena gives the impression of an inner strength and joy, which can be seen in her demeanour and the way she copes with the daily problems. She spends most

*(Above left) Gedo, a blind boy who was rescued by Annalena after being abandoned in the bush by his parents. Twelve years later he speaks four languages and plays several musical instruments.*

..............................................

*(Above right) Sister Annalena Tonelli with patients at her TB village in Wajir. By personally supervising administration of the drugs, she achieved a 96 per cent cure rate. The village has now been taken over by the government.*

..............................................

of the little free time she has at prayer, starting at dawn in a small enclosed courtyard. The floor is sand and on this there are rush mats on which to kneel. The sweet-scented frangipanis give shade to Annalena as she prays. Away from the bustle and exuberant life of the Centre, it is a place of peace and renewal.

There are now twelve children living in the Centre, although many more attend during the day. Several of the children who were there to greet us that morning I remembered meeting on previous visits. For instance, there was Gedo, the eighteen-year-old Somali boy, who contracted measles when quite young. Owing to complications he lost the sight of both eyes, and his father brought him to the hospital and abandoned him. His eyes were beyond help, but slowly he learnt braille, and went to school in Wajir. Fortunately, it was discovered that he had a talent for music and, encouraged by Annalena, he taught himself the accordion, the recorder, the drums and the guitar. He speaks good English and Italian and seems well adapted to his blindness. Annalena has arranged for him to have piano lessons in Nairobi and various schemes are afoot to enable him to carry on with his music studies. He walks round the Centre tapping his way with a long stick to prevent himself running into objects in his path. When the cool of the evening has come he will sit out in the main courtyard and start to play his accordion.

For years Gedo's parents made no contact and Annalena was unable to track them down. One day she located his mother and persuaded her to see him. Through

65

the mother she found the father, but the father was adamant; he had no use for a blind son. Another year passed before she persuaded him. It was an emotional meeting. The accomplishments of his son so impressed him that he ordered a camel feast in his honour. Like the prodigal son, Gedo was welcomed back into the family and the spirit of the tribe. This recognition was of the greatest significance for him and from that moment on he was a different person. He had become a man, confident of his status and abilities. Until that time the disability of his blindness had carried with it the burden of being an outcast from his family and people. It is only dimly that we can appreciate what sickness really means, when the trauma of rejection from the tribe is added to physical pain and weakness. In most cases those who are abandoned in the desert suffer a lingering and lonely death; it is only the lucky few who find their way to Annalena. When she goes there may be no one to save them from nature's stark realities.

Another of the children living in the Centre is Sanda Aden, a beautiful Somali girl born with a congenital defect that made her incontinent. This terrible condition soon turned her into an outcast and since she did not match up to tribal standards, she was left behind. Fortunately for her, she was gathered up by Annalena and given the love and care she so desperately needed. On one of my visits I was able to fly her to a mission hospital where we operated on her. Her return to Wajir was triumphant and her face a picture when she realized she was cured. No longer would she have to bear the embarrassment and indignity of urine dripping down her legs. She seemed to us like a miracle, as she danced a dance of joy, pirouetting with her white scarf gently flowing, bending and turning to Gedo's accompaniment. She performed an intricate Somali dance and finally returned shyly to the applause of all in the Centre.

I prepared myself to examine the line of other patients now assembled. Opposite me, sitting on a step in a small area of shade, was a carpenter, himself a cripple. Though his legs are wasted, he has strong arms and hands, and works on through the day uncomplainingly, a major asset to the Centre. He makes special boots, calipers and splints to help the children with their various disabilities. A friendly smiling man, he knows only too well the problems in the life of a cripple.

As the procession of patients came forward I tried to sort out those who would benefit from orthopaedic surgery, some of whom I had operated on before. One of the women who came in to be seen had recently been bitten by a puff adder; Annalena pointed out the mark of the bite on her foot. Everything had settled down, she had good movements in her ankle and foot and the swelling had gone. Yet she was convinced that she was a cripple for life. Nothing that was said to her would convince her to the contrary. Annalena and I discussed this trait in Somali psychology. To be bitten by a snake is like a curse, and no western mind can fully understand how all-consuming the fear is. We tried all forms of persuasion and as Annalena spoke to her in her own language, I watched, trying to understand this barrier which seemed to exclude her from any reasoning. I felt my scientific western mind confronted with that other reality, that native reality ever present in Africa in which guilt feelings are transferred and blamed on witchcraft or the supernatural or the ill-will of neighbours or family. In the case of this woman the stigma of disability had made her an outcast, acting as a confirmation of the 'curse'. Unlike Gedo and Sanda, neither the cure nor the atmosphere of the Centre could break the knowledge within her that the tribe had rejected her and that she was unclean. Without their receiving her again, a full cure could not be effected. For Africans the community and tribe are extensions of their souls. Life outside those units is, for many, inconceivable. I felt an overpowering helplessness in the face of her obdurate silence as she limped sadly away.

A little six-year-old boy with both legs in plaster was pushed up on a tricycle. His was a case of bilateral club foot. His feet have now been operated on, and the plasters are maintaining the new position. He can steer himself down the paths outside the Centre, pushed by the other children, and while this is going on he forgets his limitations.

More and more patients kept coming and we discussed their progress, watching their improvements in walking and suggesting some alternative treatments here and there. The air was cool in the courtyard as the day drew to an end. The desert roses, blood red against the white walls, danced a little in the evening breeze, moved by the hot airs from the desert. Oleanders in full bloom suddenly evoked the atmosphere of hot evenings in Italy. But the desert was only a few steps away, and its presence could be felt. There is a mystery in these dry open spaces, in the deep silences, and the distances which dissolve into the sky. It has always held a great fascination for the English, and at the time of the colonial administration, the Northern Frontier District (NFD) was a coveted post.

The children danced in the fading light as Gedo played his accordion. The plaintive music washed out into the desert spaces the heat and exhaustion of the day. We sat around listening, watching, and enjoying cold drinks. Annalena joined us, seeming to float across the courtyard in one of her long dresses, which she and her helpers always wear, out of respect for the Moslem community in which they live. Tonight it is a deep sand colour, and her long hair is knotted on top of her head. Cool and dignified she leads the way to the dining room. She says a simple grace, and then the noise and laughter bubbles forth, as everyone has something to add to the day's events.

The day is now over, and after supper the children go off to their beds. Over a cup of coffee we tell stories and reminisce. We are conscious of witnessing human tragedy being translated by courage and determination into growing human potential. As visitors, we realize that within this one room we have been privileged to see mankind in microcosm, with all its misery and heartaches, confronted at the same time by an invincible strength, stemming from the power of love.

The food is cleared away, but we sit talking, for talk is the great relaxation of the evening in this outpost where the day's work has been so hard, and where outside entertainments do not exist. I note the paradox of Annalena's presence here, and the strange situation of this community of women in an antagonistic Moslem environment. Here women are normally regarded as no better than slaves. Their work is hard in a hard country. They face a never-ending string of pregnancies, of malnutrition, of fighting for their children's survival. Perhaps the most burdensome of their circumstances is their degrading position in the community. There are even extremists who hold that women have no souls, and sometimes a Somali girl at marriage is kicked and beaten by her husband, to ensure submission in the future. Infibulation (sewing up of the vulva) is still practised. A young girl will be infibulated until her marriage, and when a man goes away he first infibulates his wife to make sure that she is faithful to him in his absence. This is also common practice in parts of Ethiopia, Somalia and the Sudan.

It does not require much imagination to understand the degradation, pain, and even sepsis that must be endured by these women, and finally the extra pain and difficulty endured at childbirth. The idea of the primitive races giving birth with ease is a total myth. Both circumcision and infibulation cause distortions and deformities, adhesions and scar tissue which add greatly to the difficulties of childbirth. Into this environment Annalena has set a community run by women for the benefit of those who, in the battle for survival, have not been considered worth saving. A sort of wonder seems to cling to the girls' faces as they begin to take part in a world of which they could not have dreamt.

The role of women in African society has been invariably subservient and one that carries with it back-breaking tasks. The cultivation, collecting and carrying of firewood and fodder, the cooking, the childbearing and child care are all their responsibility, undertaken with a minimum of material assistance. Nowadays more girls are going to school and this, more than anything, is opening their minds and imaginations to the potential of a less confined existence. With the movement gathering pace around the world in which women are challenging the limitations of their lives, there is, even in Africa, a growing realization of the contribution they can make and the greater freedom they can enjoy in these modern times. Education produces its problems however, and there is a strong tendency for families to break up. They have had a glimpse of freedom and become dissatisfied with their restricted lifestyle. The drift to the towns and the breakdown of tribal customs also results in women having children from several itinerant husbands. It is often the

*After days of walking, a camel caravan arrives at Kalacha springs in the northern Chalbi Desert. Strapped on their backs are the traditional root-fibre water bottles which will be filled for the next leg of the journey.*

grandparents who end up coping with the extra work, tending all the children, while the mother works in the town.

However, as this new trend grows, society begins to benefit from the presence of more educated women. They are quick and responsive to the new challenge. The men are more conservative and suspicious of the progress of their women. In big centres like Nairobi new careers are opening up for African women and not only in the conventional jobs such as nursing and secretarial work; they are moving into journalism, business, the professions, politics and law and finding for themselves a new life and opportunities. It is exciting, and in time, when the social upheavals have been resolved, perhaps these new women will revolutionize the future of Africa.

Education is going to be the main factor contributing to population control – an important issue in a country with the highest population growth rate in the world. Women are not going to be content to spend their whole time child bearing and child minding. Education leads to an increase in women's access to vital information which leads in turn to healthier lives for their children. Greater child survival leads paradoxically to a fall in the growth of population. This occurs in three ways. Firstly, breastfeeding itself is known to be a natural contraceptive, releasing prolactin in the mother's body and delaying the return of ovulation. Secondly as greater numbers of children survive, parents can plan more confidently the number of children they actually want rather than have extra children to compensate for the fact that one or two might die.

The third mechanism of population control is both more profound and more powerful. A husband and wife's decision to plan the number and spacing of their children is closely related to their own sense of control over their lives and circumstances. Malnutrition, illiteracy, ill health and depressed economic conditions give rise to a sense of helplessness and apathy which is not the condition in which planning of any kind, let alone family planning, can take place. If, on the other hand, progress in health and education, in political participation and economic activity, has helped create a sense that decisions can be taken, circumstances changed and lives improved, then the idea of family spacing is likely to be welcomed, as another opportunity to take more control over one's own life. It is poverty that lies at the root of the problem and prosperity that leads to reasonable control.

These factors in the lives of women in Africa are starting to make a dramatic difference to the whole issue of the population explosion, which is perhaps the most important single socio-medical problem in the continent. Already, from statistics in Asia, it can be shown that the population curve is beginning to flatten out. In Africa the results cannot yet be seen, but the evidence is growing that it is about to happen, and by the year 2030 a stable population is envisaged. An age can therefore be foreseen when women will take their rightful place in society, adding enormously to its quality and strength. In another two generations great changes will have taken place, and despite the attendant problems women will be making an incalculable contribution to African life.

We discussed this prospect well into the night. The stars above us were sharp and brilliant against the velvet depth of the sky. The pop-pop of the generator and the croak of frogs round the well were a homely comforting barrier against the surrounding wastes. The electric light bulb cast an indifferent light in a circle around us, attracting the usual cloud of insects. The moths, blinded by the light, fluttered into faces, causing a momentary disturbance, but even this ill-lit area had the friendly atmosphere of home. Gradually the air became chilly, and we were reminded how tired our limbs and minds were after such a long day. It had been an exhilarating time, and I had a haunting sense of having come close to something precious and wonderful which had been expressed in the life of this little community around us.

Daybreak, too, is a special experience in Wajir. The sky fills with birds. The sand grouse in huge flocks come in from the desert, to drink in the pools around the wells. The air is filled with the sound of wings: doves flutter across the roof tops, and join the sand grouse in their thousands. The Maribou storks, a bunch of hideous sentinels who live off the garbage of the town, stand around; I have seen one catch and swallow a pigeon in full flight, as it left the puddle at which it had been drinking.

I rose with the birds and spent a peaceful moment among the desert roses. Carmine red against the pale sand, they are among the loveliest of the desert flowers. The air was cool, and the old sun-drenched desert had a stillness that made even the stony wastes suddenly beautiful.

During the day Wajir sizzles in dry desert heat, which is not too uncomfortable. On the first days out from Nairobi visitors seem to need to drink a great deal, but slowly the body adjusts and less fluid is required. The Somalis themselves drink very little, and it is noticeable in hospital, when you are trying to persuade patients to make up for fluid loss, that they refuse to take more than a few sips.

This morning I was due to go to the government hospital to see the patients there. The doctor in charge took me round the wards to see another parade of the maimed and the blind. There were a number of cases for operation. One old man needed his prostate removing, but I found he had a very low blood count. There is no way this operation can be safely done without a blood transfusion, so the news was sent out that three pints of blood were required. Sometimes the inmates of the prison can be persuaded to donate blood, and I was hopeful it would be forthcoming.

Wajir is an example of a district hospital with only the bare minimum to carry out surgical operations. There are no frills, but the essentials are there: a simple operating table, a strip light in the ceiling, an anaesthetic machine, an electric suction pump and a selection of instrument tables, buckets and transfusion stands. The sterilizer for dressings and towels works most of the time, and the instruments are boiled in a container, heated underneath by a pressure lamp. The sterilizing of instruments takes a very long time; the room gets hotter; the flies begin to appear and are quickly sprayed.

While the theatre preparations continued, I went to speak to the Foundation on the radio, which is in the hospital administrative office. In no time I was talking to Juliet, an AMREF nursing sister who was on duty at the radio control in Nairobi. I told her I might bring a patient to Nairobi and asked her to arrange an ambulance. This contact with the outside world immediately reduces the sense of isolation. Giving her a few additional messages, I told her I would call her from the air later to tell her our exact time of arrival. We finished the ward round, and the tall doctor from western Kenya seemed to be well in control of his hospital. Of course there were many pieces of equipment which he would like to have. This time the great shortage was blood transfusion sets. I had brought up ten to keep them going, but they were temporarily out of stock at the Central Medical Stores.

Sister Teresa who has been working at the government hospital for ten years told me of more shortages. She lives at the mission not far from the hospital and has

*The old mosque in the centre of Wajir, not far from Annalena's rehabilitation centre for handicapped Somali children. Nomads and traders have been visiting Wajir for centuries on account of its famous wells.*

been a mainstay of Wajir hospital, quietly going about her work. She acts as a reliable and stable force amid the constant turnover of medical staff, who come and go, seldom remaining more than two years and often much less. She is one of the unsung heroines of northern Kenya and is the only non-African working in the hospital. She has made it her life's work and her serene, imperturbable presence gives stability and continuity to this medical outpost.

Finally, all was ready and the first patient was brought. A spinal anaesthetic was used to paralyse the patient so that he should feel nothing below the waist. The first operation proceeded well. The man was a garrulous type and talked non-stop throughout the operation. This can be rather irritating, but he was deaf to my remonstrations. The blood transfusion was successful and on this occasion the operation ran into no major problems.

On a previous visit to Wajir I was asked to help a man who had been badly mauled by a lion. Lions in the desert often become man-eaters for lack of other game, and I have often found as many as 50 per cent of hospital patients in these northern areas to be victims of lion bites. These wounds become septic almost at once and patients die quickly of septicaemia, rather than from the wound itself.

71

Hyena bites, notably in children who fall asleep herding goats and cattle, are among the worst of animal injuries. They nearly always attack the face, and the laceration of face and eyes is terrible to see. I had a small girl as a patient, who had been dragged several miles by a hyena with its teeth sunk in her face, and it took a year in hospital to rebuild her to some semblance of human form. Another young boy was flown in from Ethiopia with a similar injury, which had left him completely blind. He had already spent two years in hospital, living under a blanket – such was the horror of his facial wounds. His course of operations also took over a year to complete, during which time he learnt Swahili and braille, and finally returned to his home country, rebuilt as a human being, although blind.

The day continued with a long list of cases; the heat increased; the mound of soiled linen rose, tiredness began to take its toll and we called a halt. Annalena sent in a bucket of cold drinks and biscuits and these restored the team. While this pause continued, I went out to the ward to see that all was well. Then we started again and worked until there was no more sterile linen, and I reckoned that the nursing staff had more than enough to keep them busy.

In the afternoon, after collecting the instruments and packing up I did the final round and then drove out to the airport. The aircraft, our Cessna 206, was standing in the blazing heat and the inside of the cabin was like an oven. David hoisted himself up on to the wing and refuelled the tanks. We brought twelve gallons of petrol with us, which gave us an extra hour's flying in case we hit bad weather. We packed the aircraft and did the ground checks to see that all was well with the plane.

Annalena came to see us off. She stood, her hair and her dress blowing in the hot wind from the propellers, a strangely dominating and lonely figure against the backdrop of the desert.

We set course for Nairobi. During the flight David recounted his day with Annalena in the TB village where he had been photographing. This had caused great commotion and excitement as everyone wanted their pictures taken. A photograph makes a great impression when a person has not seen his face in a mirror, so David had to make many promises to send back copies to them all before going on to visit the wells, and photograph the camels not far from Wajir.

The Lorian swamp, fed by the Uaso Nyiro river to the west, lay below us. This area was once a great marsh where the biggest elephants in Africa were found. Today it is almost dry, with a trickle of water flowing through it, as it becomes part of the surrounding desert. Only in times of exceptional rainfall does it revert to its old lushness. The elephants have all disappeared.

Habaswein, a tiny village on the road up to Wajir, passed below us. It was from this isolated airstrip that I watched the total eclipse of the sun in 1973. We had flown down from Wajir, where my eldest son was Medical Officer at the time, to watch this singular event. The sun turned black, but was surrounded by a burning-white halo. The desert fell silent as the birds began mistakenly to roost and the cattle made for home. An uneasy grey light drained all the colour from the desert and we watched in awed silence as the sun slowly regained strength.

*(Opposite) A beautiful Gabbra girl photographed while loading water bottles on to her camels at Kalacha springs. The keys hanging from her necklace are only for decoration.*

CHAPTER FOUR

# ISLANDS OF THE ZINJ

····················································

T he little jetty came in sight round a corner of the footpath that led through the mangrove swamps. Beyond the jetty, at which an old motorized dhow was drawn up, was the coastline of Lamu Island, with the romantic old pink and white buildings of the town lining the waterfront, decaying yet venerable, shimmering over the intervening choppy little channel of sea. I had flown down from Nairobi following a call from our flying doctor, Anne Spoerry, who needed my help with an emergency. Already feeling the humid heat, I loaded the baggages into the dhow and set off from Manda Island where I had landed, across to Lamu Island's main jetty.

There was much coming and going at the little port. Several dhows were unloading cargoes and passengers, and it was necessary for me to hump my bags of surgical instruments over two or three boats before reaching the steep steps on which I could already see Anne waiting to help me. On dry land at last we wove an intricate route through the narrow streets, avoiding donkeys carrying huge blocks of coral, people with hand carts, women in the black overall garments of the coast which only allow their eyes to show, vendors of every kind of fruit and sweetmeat, and up the hill to a friend's house behind the gigantic old prison fort.

Historical and dirty with a raffish charm, the island of Lamu is the site of settlements which date back nearly two thousand years. Only twelve miles long by five miles wide, this little island consists mainly of high sand dunes and waving palm trees, but at the northern end are two towns, Lamu town and Shela, separated by one and a half miles of beach. It lies some seventy miles south of the Somali border and Lamu town itself dates back at least a thousand years, and was one of a number of trading ports from which ivory, rhino horn and slaves were exported for centuries. This Afro-Arab civilization was originally founded by the Persians well before the birth of Christ, but Lamu itself only reached a peak of prosperity, a golden age, during the seventeenth and eighteenth centuries.

The island is difficult to reach by road, the only route running north from Malindi to Garsen – about seventy miles of dirt road – where one crosses the Tana River on a hand-operated ferry. Over the river the road winds through a jungle of Mbogo and Mkoma trees and a wide natural depression which becomes a flood plain when the Tana overflows its banks. It then continues for a further seventy miles to the Makowe Jetty which serves the islands of the Lamu archipelago, Lamu, Manda and Pate. The easy way to reach the island is, however, by aeroplane and many visitors arrive this way avoiding the long and difficult road journey.

Lamu town does not face the open sea, but looks across at Manda Island with its seaboard obscured in mangrove swamps. All the islands are surrounded by mangroves, the poles of which are harvested systematically and form part of the islands' trade with Arabia.

It is not the island itself that is remarkable, but the unique character of the people who live there. Their culture is very old, and of mixed origin. Although Islamic by religion, its customs derive solely from the culture of the Swahili, a people of mixed Bantu and Arab blood, who enjoyed prosperity and political power here many centuries ago. Moslem customs are superimposed on old Bantu superstitions, similar to those of the Turkana and other desert tribes of the north, while other customs date back for centuries to origins as remote as Russian and Arab trading links from the Middle East. What has survived is unique, and stepping into Lamu is like stepping into another age as well as another world.

The Swahilis in the past had great influence up and down the coast. They gave the whole area of East Africa their language as a lingua franca which makes it possible for the many East African peoples to communicate today. I have been as far away as the western Congo, and understood Swahili words in conversation. The Swahili are lovers of ceremony and processions. On great occasions, for weddings and festivals, even to this day, processions throng the street led by the Shogas, or male prostitutes who dress as women and paint their faces to attract attention. They dance and play in bands as drummers for the occasion. Lights and bright clothes make a brilliant scene against the backcloth of the warm darkness, as they pass down the narrow alleys singing and dancing. The Shogas appear to play the part of eunuchs in the community. Women feel safe with them, and the men also do not resent the contact of the Shogas with their womenfolk. They are carriers of messages, often between lovers, illicit or otherwise.

Another interesting idiosyncrasy of this culture is its treatment of the mentally disturbed, or those supposed to be bewitched or possessed of devils. The spirit dancers are called and with singing and dancing they will try to call on the spirits to heal the possessed one. Meanwhile the 'patient' if a man will dress up as a woman, and if a woman will dress as a man. They will act out their fantasies expressing all the horror, distress and lament of a human soul. The whole community will gather round, not out of curiosity, but to assist the patient in his acting. The family also joins in to encourage and enlarge on the fantasies which are being enacted. Such

*(Opposite) Example of intricate local plaster craft in an eighteenth-century Lamu house. The walls of these houses are very thick, rendering them relatively cool during the often oppressive heat of the day. Lamu is the site of settlements dating back over 1000 years to a time when the land between the upper Nile and Mozambique was known as the land of the 'Zinj'.*

*(Previous page) A fishing dhow sails peacefully across a broad channel separating two of the larger islands in the Lamu archipelago. The only access to these remote communities is by dhow or by plane.*

ceremonies have interesting parallels in the theories of Jung, who would undoubtedly have understood their significance, expressing as they do the female element in male psychology and the male element in the female.

During Malindi, the great festival to celebrate the Prophet's birth, as many as ten thousand Moslems come to Lamu. There are great processions, day and night. The streets are decorated with bunting, there is dancing along the waterfront with the beating of drums, the blowing of huge horns and the banging of cymbals. The whole town comes alive, the stench of open drains increases, every house bulges with humanity and cholera stalks the street. During the day stick dances are held, which are really fights with sticks to decide who is the best man there. These fights are not too serious and are often held at weddings, when it is customary and considered polite to let the bridegroom win. Pepo dances are held all night when the pepos or spirits, also known as Jinis, are appeased by the performance, drums continue to roll, and the weird music of the horns and cymbals brings the excitement to a hysterical pitch. People are dressed in all manner of fancy-dress and make-up is heavily used especially by the males and the Shogas, all masquerading as women. Such festivities, which are frequent in Lamu, preserve and transmit the old culture down the years.

Nowadays the town is a historical monument which is rapidly decaying. The old houses cluster together. Built with walls of coral two feet thick, they consist of a series of alcoves, rather than rooms, about eight to ten feet wide, their width being controlled by the length of the mangrove poles which are the rafters for floors and ceilings. Many of them are three stories high, with precipitous staircases which end on a flat roof where much of the life of the community goes on.

For a number of years this isolated community has been served by the Government Health Service, but the long distances and the problems of getting round the area have severely hampered the district medical officer in performing his duties. Now, however, by installing a number of airstrips on the neighbouring islands, it has been possible to set up clinics in outlying villages. The Flying Doctor Service from Nairobi provides the aircraft, pilot and doctor in the form of Dr Anne Spoerry and her plane. She is responsible for setting up such clinics, in conjunction with the District Medical Officer, and is often accompanied by a medical team. This service is one which she has pioneered in many remote areas of Kenya, and her exhausting schedule includes the Northern Frontier District of Kenya, Rusinga Island and Lake Victoria, Maasailand and, of course, the Lamu islands.

Anne is a colourful person. Of French-Swiss origin, she was a member of the French Resistance during the Second World War which ended for her with three years in a concentration camp. This has produced in her a hardiness which keeps her pushing out the frontiers of medicine in the most remote parts of Africa. She combines a volatile Gallic temperament with outstanding courage and determination. She has a farm in the Subukia valley in up-country Kenya, but her holiday home is Lamu. In the little village of Shela, along the coast from Lamu town, Anne has a complex of three or four old Arab houses which she has restored, and in which she has collected many Swahili artifacts of historical value.

*Face of an old Lamu inhabitant who was born on the island of Zanzibar before the turn of the century. Amongst the dusty memorabilia in his sitting room was a faded portrait of King George VI.*

Since we installed a solar-powered radio network in the Lamu District, the Medical Officer has been able to keep in touch with the island outstations. He can now keep them supplied with essential materials and is able to provide emergency facilities when needed. It enables him, for instance, to organize the immunization of groups of children, give advice on hygiene and training to their mothers, and to supply the necessary drugs. But it is the occasional emergency, as in the case on hand, which really demonstrates the value of radio communications, for here it takes on a life-saving role.

Reaching the roof top of our friend's house that morning, I felt the community huddled around me, carrying on age-old chores. A woman was combing thick black hair on a verandah a hundred yards away. A man in a bright kikoi lay still asleep on his bed. A tourist sat on a wall basking in the sun. Two cats began yowling on another roof top; radios blared Swahili music; Moslem chants and Christian hymns vied with each other from below. A row of washing, full blown with wind, danced among the tops of date and coconut palms. A jihazi dhow raised its sail and left the crowded quay for the open sea; a man in the bows opened a black umbrella against the growing heat of the sun. Donkeys edged their way down the narrow passages that divide Lamu houses and serve the town for streets.

As I sat down, sipping tamarind juice after the exertions of the climb, Dr Spoerry explained the emergency I had come to deal with. Anne Spoerry has been a colleague of mine since 1964. She sat opposite me, a dumpy figure in loose men's clothing, and ran her hand through grey short-cropped hair.

'This woman', she said, 'has been in labour seventy-two hours. She was moved over to Lamu from Pate in a dug-out canoe this morning. The journey took many hours and she arrived totally moribund.

'If it weren't for the radio,' Anne continued, 'she would be a dead woman.' I could not help but agree with her.

'We'd better get moving,' I said. 'Have you managed to get any blood for transfusion?'

'Yes,' said Anne. 'She was in a desperate condition and I have already set up a drip.'

In the tiny street below we managed to obtain a hand cart into which we piled the cases of instruments and medical supplies. The man pulling the cart raced ahead, oblivious of other people, shouting 'Gari! Gari!' People jumped on to doorsteps to avoid the vehicle, and we followed on foot in its wake, breathing the foetid air of open drains.

The hospital is on a slight rise behind the old prison. Patients sit about in small pools of shade made by palms and bougainvillea bushes. A disreputable array of cats roll in the hot dust, and slither along in the shade of the walls, waiting expectantly at the kitchen entrance.

A bright little nursing sister in starched cap and apron greeted us as we entered the ward. Some twenty patients lay under doubtful grey sheets and greyer blankets. They looked dully at the ceiling and the walls, and regarded us silently as we came to the bed of the dying woman. I could see at once that she was deeply shocked. The first laboratory test on her blood showed that she had only 12 per cent of her blood

*An old lady on remote Pate Island reading the Koran. Her seventeenth-century gold jewellery serves as a reminder of the great days of Pate and the civilization of the Zinj.*

*(Above) A coastal dhow approaching Lamu harbour under full sail. Dhows like these have plied up and down the East African coast for thousands of years with little change in their basic design.*

..........................................

*(Previous page) Dhows at anchor on the Lamu waterfront at dawn. Nowadays, Lamu's biggest export is mangrove poles which are used for scaffolding and construction work in the Middle East. The poles are transported by dhow up the coast to Arabia.*

..........................................

volume left. This was so low that Anne felt she must shortly die unless blood could be given to her in considerable quantities. The clinical officer had therefore been busy and had laid in six more units of blood for her. It is not an easy task to persuade people to give blood unless they are relatives.

I bent down to examine the form on the bed. The body of the child lay between the woman's legs while the head was still lodged in the abdomen. It appeared to be a case of hydrocephalus, or water on the brain, in which the foetal head was too large to pass through the birth canal. I could detect a long rent in the uterus; blood pressure was unrecordable, since the woman had already lost almost all her blood. I could feel no pulse; she was cold, sweaty and gasping.

We raised the foot of her bed and shortly after the second unit of blood arrived I decided to set up a second transfusion in her other arm. Since the veins were all totally collapsed there was no chance of using a needle: I had to cut down under the skin to find a vein into which I could insert a cannula. With this tied in position, the blood, now cross-matched, began to flow in. The blood had to be run in fast through two drips in order to replace rapidly the great loss of blood she had sustained. There was not much more we could do except watch and wait.

Not very hopeful about the outcome, I went out to see the husband, and did not minimize the extreme gravity of the position. He told me his wife had previously had six children without any trouble. Why should she have trouble now? I explained about the baby's head so that he could understand the mechanical problem. On returning to the ward I could see no improvement; her life seemed to be ebbing away. There was nothing else we could do. The midday heat was growing in strength, the doorway was filled with relatives who had come over in the boat with her. I shooed them away and told them they were obstructing the work of the nursing staff. Looking decidedly resentful they nevertheless retreated a few paces. I shut the door. Was there any more blood coming? I certainly could not think of operating on her in her present condition; it was out of the question.

The medical assistant came to the rescue. He hurried off to the prison compound and asked for volunteers to give blood. Induced by the promise of being excused some fatigue or other, the prisoners' response was immediate and sufficient for our needs. Thanks to the innate toughness of the woman, she was still hanging on to her life. I asked a nurse to sponge her gently. There was a flicker of her eyelids as the sponge was wiped across her face. Good news came that another two units of blood would be with us shortly.

It was an agonizing time simply waiting and hoping. The two new bottles of blood were put up as the old ones were finished. The patient was still alive; the blood was running faster. The nurse thought she felt a pulse; I could not be sure. The skin was still cold and clammy. Over the next hour a small but marked improvement could be detected with the eye of faith. The nurse took our instruments down to the theatre for something to do while the vigil continued.

The woman was definitely showing signs of life. Could we keep the supply of blood coming? This was the vital issue. I spoke to the husband again. Had he any relatives in Lamu or close friends who could help. He went off to consult with the relatives outside. I was worried that the woman might start bleeding again from the rent in the uterus as her blood pressure rose. We hung on: she was now really better. We decided to move her to the theatre and wait. Very gently and slowly she was transferred to a trolley and down to the theatre. The anaesthetist felt it was a great risk to give her an anaesthetic. I could only agree with him. What was the alternative? There wasn't one. All we had to debate was the timing of the operation – not too early and not too late.

When the eighth pint was received I felt we could take the risk; the circulation was much improved, the woman had stopped sweating and her skin was now warmer. I went to see the husband and told him that I would probably have to remove the uterus. He refused to allow this. I told him I could not be responsible for his wife's life if he didn't change his mind. Unable to move him, I found a local nurse who said she would try to persuade him. Eventually he signed the consent form and we could begin.

The woman's husband was neither callous nor obstinate. In his view a wife was essentially a producer of children who were his wealth, his security in old age and most important of all his immortality. It was reasonable, therefore, that he should want to preserve his wife's ability to bear children; probably to him a woman who could not bear children was a liability to the family, another mouth to feed. In this Swahili community women are usually in an insecure position. A husband can divorce a woman by saying 'I divorce you' three times in front of a witness. The woman then has to leave her husband's house and make her own way either in business or prostitution or by remarriage. The children are the property of the

husband. Often women do remarry their original husbands. It is customary, however, for them to marry someone else in between. As a result of these customs, women do not trust their husband's household at the vulnerable time of childbirth, and always return to their mothers, however remote or unsuitable their homes may be.

Now that the operation was to go ahead, the anaesthetic was clearly going to be the trickiest part. It was done in masterly fashion. The anaesthetist looked up and said, 'When you start please be as quick as you can. This is one of the rare occasions when speed is vital. I want her off the table as soon as possible.'

The operation began; the blood was pink and obviously well oxygenated; the transfusions were still working without a hitch. It was hard work with the temperature in the theatre well over 100°F. Quickly I removed the hydrocephalic head of the child which was free in the abdominal cavity. There was no doubt about the water on the brain; the head was at least twice the normal size. Then I looked at the uterus – it had a rupture in it about ten inches long. The decision to remove the uterus had to be made now. Her condition was still improving. As quickly as I could I went through the stages of a hysterectomy. It was not technically difficult and soon we were sewing up. Her condition stayed much the same. We left her on the operating table after the dressings had been put on; there was no point in moving her. I went out to see the husband and told him the news without raising his hopes too high.

We decided to let her have all the available blood though we cut the speed of the transfusion a little. An hour or so later we moved her to her bed. There was nothing more I could do except write out the post-operative instructions and hope for the best. We walked down to the hotel where Anne had booked us rooms. The time was late, but the staff had kindly waited up to give us some food. A bottle of beer before the food came was particularly welcome. It was a hot sultry night and we had lost a lot of fluid. Before going to bed I walked up the hill and saw our patient. It seemed she would recover. Surgeons tend to remember their successes and conveniently forget their failures. On this occasion I marvelled at the stamina of the woman; she deserved to live.

The hazardous existence of this woman and her community made me starkly aware of the problems of life in this area. By far the greatest problem of this unique community is its isolation; but it is this same isolation that has enabled it to survive more or less intact over so many hundreds of years. Western civilization has not made many inroads into the culture of the islands, and the Moslem culture from the East has overlaid much Bantu belief. It is true that in the sixties an invasion of hippies, who squatted in the empty decaying houses, brought drugs, the aftermath of which is destroying some of the inhabitants to this day. Nowadays government intervention from the mainland, in the form of laws and regulations, is intruding on the whole in a beneficial manner.

*(Opposite above) Carved from solid ivory, this seventeenth-century siwa from Pate Island was used to warn other island communities of impending attack during the heyday of Zinj. This siwa is one of Africa's most priceless art treasures.*

*(Opposite below) A procession surging along the waterfront during the Moslem festival of Malindi which commemorates the birth of the prophet Muhammad— the Islamic equivalent of Christmas.*

The coast is one of the worst areas for malaria and in Lamu it is the most serious and most common disease. A particularly severe type of malaria originates in the hot, humid coastal strip. Recently the mosquito has shown a tendency to become immune to the chloroquin-based drugs which proved so effective ten years ago. As a result dosage has been increased, which in its turn begins to affect the human being adversely. A malaria-carrying mosquito can only live a quarter of a mile from water, which accounts for the fact that malaria is found in lakeside areas, or in towns where long-standing puddles of water or tanks holding stagnant water give the mosquito the opportunity to breed.

Research workers are hoping one day to produce a vaccine. AMREF, too, has a research team which is working specifically on malaria and the growing resistance of the disease to anti-malarials. The doctors of the team hold that the best way to prevent malaria is to be under a mosquito net between the hours of 11 pm and 6 am, for it is between these hours that the female anopheles mosquito, a tiny mosquito that makes no noise and which carries the disease, comes out to feed.

Malaria is still a major scourge in the tropics, killing an estimated three million people per year. It produces high fever, dehydration, cerebral invasion, breakdown of the kidneys (black water) and many other serious symptoms. It can be eliminated from a township by constant spraying of the breeding grounds, or the elimination of standing water. Vaccination will eventually become the method of control, but it will never be as easy to eliminate as smallpox, because it is borne by an insect which will be very difficult to destroy.

Tourists are daily intruding into the lives of the people, so that the young men are leaving the time-honoured occupation of fishing for the profitable occupation of ferrying tourists around in their dhows. But the numbers of tourists are controlled by limited accommodation, distance and difficulties of transport so that generally speaking only relatively few people reach Lamu, and almost none reach the outer islands. Time here has stood still and only a slow natural decay is apparent. But the problem is there and isolation, the preserver of culture, can also be a threat to human life when an emergency arises.

Anne Spoerry's programme provides some idea of the difficulties which face anyone trying to provide a medical service in this area. She visits the islands once in six weeks, and carries out an immunization programme designed to prevent disease and instruct the women in childcare. Preventative medicine seems to be by far the best course to take compared with the difficulties of dealing with disease in extremis, with all the complications of transport, distance and the sea. To reach the places in which she has chosen to concentrate her services, Anne has to fly to one of the small strips, which we made a few years ago in cooperation with the government. Then proceeding on foot, she and her staff have to tramp for up to an hour over hot sand, through mangrove swamps, under an unremitting sun. At one place, Faza on Pate Island, the aircraft lands at Kizingitingi. The expedition then has to transfer to a boat and chug to Faza Port, often to find that the tide prevents a landing and a wait of up to four hours can ensue. Having arrived at Faza, a further hour's walk is necessary to the clinic. One can understand the difficulties of such a journey for someone critically ill, strapped to a makeshift stretcher, perhaps loaded on top of a donkey for the long ride to the sea. At times it is not possible to round the northern end of Manda Island and pass through the channel to Lamu or the mainland. In addition, an eight-hour boat journey has to be faced if there is no aeroplane on Pate Island; but the dozen or so airstrips in the area have made the evacuation of emergencies possible and the radio, which now connects several of the government clinics, makes it possible to summon help when necessary.

This year I counted the Lamu district clinics which Anne plans to hold. Her list numbers twenty-three different places visited over twelve months; some of these are visited twice and half of them involve an hour-long walk. And this only includes the clinics she holds in the coastal area. To these have to be added those held in northern Kenya and her visits to Rusinga Island in Lake Victoria. It is an enormous task involving great physical effort, organization, improvisation and the human sympathy which is the mainspring of all Anne's work.

The other day during one of her long hot walks, Anne came to a small hamlet hidden among the sand dunes. An old woman emerged shrouded in her buibui, the black overall garment the women wear which enables them to cover their faces when a man appears. Anne wondered what she could be wanting from her, and prepared herself to face another problem. The old woman, however, held out her hands and in them was a bowl of brown eggs.

Anne stopped and asked in a surprised voice, 'Are these for me? What have I done to be offered such a beautiful present?'

'It was my daughter whom you flew to Mombasa when she was in childbirth, and who died there.'

Anne remembered. A young girl, who had reached a critical stage of eclampsia in childbirth, had arrived in Lamu in an open dug-out canoe. There were insufficient facilities to deal with such an emergency in Lamu hospital. Anne therefore decided, late though it was, with big cumulus clouds piled high in the sky, to fly immediately to Mombasa with the girl. She managed to reach Mombasa hospital, but the girl died during the night.

This touching offering was to celebrate not a success but a failure, a failure which demonstrated a singular care for human life. It would have been so easy to claim the lateness of the hour, the expense of flying all that way, the little chance the girl had of survival. But it was the care for one unknown girl that defeated all these rational arguments, and it was the care that was now recognized by the gift of eggs.

On another occasion Anne was in her house in Shela one Sunday afternoon. Her top-storey bedroom, looking out over waving palm trees and the sea, contains the high frequency radio connecting her with a number of island clinics and Lamu hospital. She was lying on the bed, draped in mosquito netting, when the radio started calling her. It was the hospital secretary from Lamu. He had received news of a bad accident at Kiunga on the Somali border, some sixty nautical miles north of Lamu. The District Officer and the Chief with a few attendants had been travelling at top speed in a Land Rover. They had met head on with another Land Rover, also travelling very fast. Six men were badly injured; they had to send help before nightfall.

With a great effort Anne roused herself from the humid heat of the afternoon. She snatched up her first aid kit and a simple stretcher she kept in the house. She sent a servant running to the nearby hotel for the use of their speedboat, for the old diesel boats that might, or might not, be at the jetty took half an hour to reach Manda Island and the airport. The speedboat arrived as Anne, with her load, carried by a line of servants, reached the jetty. In a few minutes they were loaded and speeding across the channel between Lamu and Manda, the spray flying in a great arc either side of the boat.

Sunday afternoon at the hospital had proved unfruitful for the hospital secretary. He had been unable to raise any medical supplies, but he came himself to help Anne. She saw from afar his familiar figure on Manda jetty and as they drew alongside he ran down the steps to help unload and hand Anne ashore. He had organized a wooden cart and some boys to help carry the equipment to the airstrip which was ten minutes' walk inland. Miraculously they were airborne by four o'clock. Speeding up the coast along the peacock-coloured shoreline, white-fringed by surf and sand, they reached the tiny airstrip at 5.15 pm.

They radioed ahead and now the local clinic staff were there with half the population, willing to help and full of curiosity. The officials made a way through the crowd and they hurried to the clinic where the injured men lay.

The District Officer was the worst injured, with head injuries and fractured pelvis and arm. They loaded him on to the stretcher, while first aid treatment was given to others. The Chief had sustained a fractured elbow and arm and the others had cuts and minor fractures. They were loaded into the plane and were off again by 6 pm. Again radioing ahead they were met on Manda by local help. Everyone had turned out to lend a hand, and it was in large part due to the local people that the patients arrived in Lamu in a short time. Lanterns were held high in the gathering dark, as the stretcher was loaded onto the swinging boat. Black backs glistened with sweat as the engine was roused to life, and they pushed off towards the lights of Lamu, which glowed suddenly ahead in the already black night.

The same chief who was involved in this accident was in a convoy which was shot up by Shifta a few months later. His Land Rover had twenty-six bullets in it, when the Shifta caught him and his election team in a sand drift on the same road. On that occasion the wounded were not so fortunate. One man died as they limped to Kiunga on the rims of punctured tyres. From there they loaded the wounded on to an open boat, and another man died on the sea between Kiunga and Lamu. The last man died on the way to Mombasa the next day. This incident serves to demonstrate the extent to which the people of the islands live in fear of the Shifta. They do not venture on to the mainland if they can help it and whereas in the past many of them cultivated rich farms on the mainland, these have all been deserted.

Increasing poverty, the second major problem of the area, is also due to the decline of Lamu as a port for Arabian and Middle Eastern trade. When in 1840, Said Said, the reigning sultan, moved his court to Zanzibar, many of the rich moved with him and trade and influence followed. Many of the mainland farms which provided much of the wealth of Lamu, growing simsim and sorghum for eastern markets, were reliant on slaves. At about the same time that the Sultan moved to Zanzibar, the emancipation of the slaves was brought about and this made the mainland shambas increasingly uneconomical. The prosperity of Lamu has never returned and the final blow was dealt by the arrival of the British, who chose Mombasa as their deep water port from which to open up the interior. Lamu exists now in poverty and isolation, a relic of the past. However, with modern communications reaching the islands, and the inland government including them in the life of Kenya as a nation, tiny shoots of new activity are beginning to show.

One of the outstanding examples of this new life is the beautiful little museum, with its relics of the golden past and the trade of the islands with the far and near eastern world. It is carefully cherished, with a growing library for the local people.

The problems of Lamu are, in microcosm, the problems of much of Africa – isolation and poverty – and superimposed on this ancient patchwork is the philosophy of life derived from the Islamic and African religions. Adversity or success is the will of Allah or Mungu, and humanity is helpless in the face of such towering odds. This deep, all-pervading acceptance is enervating in the extreme and the basis of an apathy which the climate exacerbates.

Yet the opposite is also true, and such acceptance could offer much to western civilization to relieve the growing tensions of modern life. In Africa problems are meant to be lived with, whereas in the western world they are to be solved. Perhaps there is a balance between these two views which we have not yet achieved, which would be of benefit to both continents.

The African way of thought also embodies one vital difference from western attitudes, which is crucial to our way of viewing the world. Africans externalize the happenings of their lives, whereas we internalize them. For example, whilst we would fall off our bicycle, the African would say that the bicycle threw him. So for him it is the day that is unpropitious, the ancestors who have some grudge which they are working out, or some ill-wisher who has bewitched an enemy, a barren wife or the scanty crops. The sequence of western logic, of cause and effect is generally not recognized or applied. This attitude has had and could still have a profound effect on the future of Africa.

*In the absence of any cars or roads, Dr Anne Spoerry is often obliged to travel in a small dhow from one community to another while carrying out her medical duties.*

The attitude is a side effect of the African's consciousness of himself as an extended soul. His soul is in his family, his relatives alive or dead, his goods and land and cattle which are all part of, and make up his total being. Here the West could learn a lesson, for we have become so isolated in our militant individualism that we have lost all connection with our natural environment, no longer respecting the companion flora and fauna which enrich our way through life, and abusing the earth and its multitudinous forms of life as never before.

It is because of this abuse of environment that a powerful lobby known as the 'Greens' has grown up in many countries in the West to protest against the policies and way of life which have led to acid rain, the destruction of forests, the pollution of lakes and seas with industrial waste and the covering of the country with acres of new concrete every year. In most of Africa we have so far escaped these forms of pollution, but our treatment of the land and forests is part and parcel of the same lack of concern for our environment. The growing brown stain in the Indian Ocean at the mouth of our rivers is ample evidence of our numerous soil erosion problems. Large areas of bush have been cut down to make charcoal for the Middle East. In the absence of proper agricultural methods the desert encroaches year by year.

Problems such as these were hotly debated as we sat on Anne's rooftop in Shela. Indeed the predicament of Africa today is a never-ending subject of conversation for those of us who have adopted the country, problems and all. Anne poured out the wine. The sun fell suddenly and dramatically behind the feathered top of a palm tree. The sky was full of a green light which fell in a liquid pathway across the water. The lights of Shela bloomed one by one. The moon rose, the thinnest of porcelain cups holding in it the deep blue dark. The wine flowed and our thoughts brimmed over into talk, from which new ideas came one upon the other, laced with enthusiasm, dampened by the heat. A zinging mosquito reminded us sharply of mortality, the plop of the waves soothed and refreshed and dreamy eyes became fixed on the open sea.

*The old Friday mosque at Shela on Lamu Island. Shela was a thriving town during the great days of the ivory trade in the eighteenth and nineteenth centuries.*

# CHAPTER FIVE

# MAYDAY!
# MAYDAY!

······································

**M**ayday! Mayday!' the pilot's call for help, is one of the most crucial communications issued in the modern world.

To understand the significance of such communications in Africa one has only to picture the vast distances, the sparse and scattered populations in many areas, the lack of roads or means of penetrating into the desert and bush areas, to realize that when disaster strikes, there is, likely as not, no one to help. Throughout the greater part of the continent there are no telephones at all. In big towns like Nairobi the telephone works in a somewhat desultory fashion, and even in Kenya, where standards are higher than in most places, contact with other towns can be difficult, although satellites have done a lot to improve international communication.

One of the most distressing things to be seen in any African hospital are the patients with untreated disease who would have been cured if they had come to hospital earlier. When, however, one remembers the distances they have travelled on foot, or in some makeshift hand cart, one realizes why the condition has to be desperately serious before such a journey is undertaken. This is the reason why most African hospitals are like a museum of extreme conditions of disease seldom seen anywhere else. Many cancers only reach hospital in their terminal stages. In a country where road accidents and trauma, particularly burns and injuries from wild animals, are prolific one can imagine the advanced septicaemias, the badly fused fractures and the contortions due to burn contractures which present such a staggering picture in the hospital wards of Africa today.

Communications in the broadest sense, therefore, are the key to improving the health of the African community. They also offer a unique possibility of improving health with the minimum of expenditure, for the telephone, radio, aeroplane and car can bring an instant answer and immediate support in an emergency. At the same time they can diffuse information and education to the rural populations of Africa, familiarizing them with the uses of modern medicine in a way which should benefit the whole population.

When I first came to Africa in 1947 it seemed to me that the use of modern communications was the single most important thing which could relieve suffering, increase the possibility of survival and extend the health services at relatively little cost. The radio network was thus the first project undertaken by AMREF as far back as 1958.

One evening I was working late in the office and I heard our radio room suddenly spring to life.

'Roger, this is Foundation Control.' I could hear the voice of the nurse on duty down the corridor struggling to make herself heard over the crackling radio. A distorted reply came back through a blanket of atmospherics.

'This is Tsavo Camp calling. Tsavo Camp. Tsavo Camp. Over.'

'I am reading you, Tsavo,' the nurse's voice replied. 'What is your problem?'

'We have a case of snake bite and wish to ask a doctor's advice.'

'Roger, please stand by. I will call a doctor.' At that moment I rounded the corner of the corridor and appeared in the radio room. 'Oh, Dr Wood,' said Juliet. 'Could you give some advice over the radio? It's an emergency. Snake bite at Tsavo.'

I took up the mike and spoke into it. 'Michael Wood here. Can I help?'

'Dr Wood,' came the reply, 'I am in charge of Tsavo Camp and a young boy has been bitten on the ankle by a black mamba. He is very shocked and in a lot of pain. Should I give him anti-snake venom?'

'Stand by,' I replied, as I thought for a moment. Tsavo was four hours' drive away and it was already growing dark. A plane would find it difficult to get there before nightfall. The boy was in shock and would probably react badly to the anti-venom.

In cases such as these the severity of the bite often depends on whether it was a glancing blow or a real bite, when the venom would have injected deeply into the tissue. I knew too that fear plays a very large part in how patients react to the shock, and perhaps if the boy knew we were coming he would remain calm for a while.

Black mamba bites are often fatal. The venom is neurotoxic and can paralyse the muscles of respiration. Large intravenous doses of anti-venom can be given, but this sometimes causes 'anaphylactic shock' which can be more serious than the snake bite, and indeed can cause death unless the patient is in a hospital where such an emergency can be dealt with instantly. It is sometimes said that anti-venom causes more problems than the venom itself, so I replied with some caution.

'Tsavo,' I called, 'if the boy is already shocked, I would not advise you to give the anti-venom as it might produce an alarming reaction which could only be coped with in hospital. If you have any hydrocortisone give that and keep him as still as possible.'

'Yes, we have some,' came the reply. 'Can you come and fetch him?'

I gave instructions for the administration and dosage of the drug and painkillers. 'We will send a plane at once,' I concluded. 'Have as many cars as you can on the airstrip with their lights on. Place them one at either end, and the rest down the sides, in a chevron pattern, facing into the wind so as not to dazzle the pilot. Keep the cars well back from the strip to give the pilot room to land.'

The flight to Tsavo Camp takes about an hour. No visible human habitation marks the course. Over miles of semi-desert and bush, a sand river snaking its way from a group of high hills leads to the wide soda flats of Lake Amboseli on the

*(Previous page) Flamingoes take flight as a Flying Doctor plane skims the surface of Lake Magadi in the Rift Valley en route for Shombole near the Tanzanian border. The aircraft is reflected in the glassy waters of the lake.*

starboard wing. At night the camp would be difficult to find, but the Camp Manager left all his lights on, the cars were lined up as I described, and the pilot did not lose his course. He came straight in to land with great precision to find a Land Rover waiting with the patient lying with his feet out over the tail gate. The AMREF nurse who had accompanied the pilot fixed up an intravenous drip with adrenalin and more hydrocortisone in it without moving the boy from the car. When the drip had had some effect on his blood pressure, he was moved gently into the aircraft and as he appeared to be holding his own, with no paralysis setting in, they took off for Nairobi, into a night with no stars, and only the feeble gleam behind the instruments to take them the hundred miles back to a safe hospital bed. In this case two types of communication, air and radio, had been used to life-saving effect.

The outcome was not so happy on another occasion. I was in a hospital in the bush at a place called Ortum when a man employed by Jonathan Leakey was bitten by a mamba while catching snakes. He was admitted ten to twelve hours after a long journey. Jonathan gave him enormous doses of anti-venom intravenously believing correctly that it was the only way of saving his life. He was admitted in the evening after we had finished an operating list. He was cold, clammy and almost pulseless. We transfused him, gave him adrenalin and hydrocortisone into his drip, and put his bed on blocks so his head was kept low. We stayed with him all night, but he died at dawn without rallying at all. It was a case of anaphylactic shock which proved to be irreversible.

Africa, and in particular Kenya, is fast making use of modern technology to improve communications. In Kenya we have not only television in Nairobi but also satellite telecommunication which has made contact with the outside world so good that many people think it easier to phone New York than nearby Nairobi. As I fly over the Rift Valley I see below me the flower-like faces of the great satellite saucers lifted to the sky, scanning the ultimate blue of outer space. Planted there in the old earth of Africa, perhaps the oldest land surface in the world, surrounded by mile upon mile of semi-desert and bush, they are strange flora indeed. But it will be from these satellites that we shall one day be able to link up the doctor or specialist in Nairobi to the patient and clinical officer many miles off in the bush. Such a device would save the patient hours of painful and uncomfortable travel, diagnosis could be made easier, and instant action taken if it was necessary to bring the patient in quickly. In these days when fuel is scarce and expensive, unnecessary travel has to be avoided. Radio, telephones and television will help us increasingly to overcome the problem of distance and, so to speak, bring the patient into the consulting room without moving him.

A few years ago I was in the Arctic at Inuvik, at the mouth of the McKenzie River, and witnessed this new type of telephonic communication, when it was possible to see both patient and doctor although they were 2,000 miles apart. Likewise, in Africa, I envisage a time when we will be able to see our patient in the bush, and have the case history read to us by the nurse or clinical officer on the spot. This will make diagnosis at a distance possible and even finally with a computer attachment we shall be able to make diagnosis more reliable. When I remember the many patients I have seen brought in on a ramshackle stretcher on the back of a donkey, driven hundreds of miles in the back of a pick up with a broken back, paddled for hours in an open dug-out canoe, I know that this kind of technology will be a merciful adjunct to medicine in Africa.

In Canada the consultant sitting in his office in Montreal could see the patient in Inuvik on the screen on his desk and listen to the nurse describe the patient's symptoms. He could ask the nurse questions, prescribe for the patient and ask to be kept informed. Evacuation may be required but often it is best to leave the patient quiet and undisturbed provided he is somewhere where treatment can be carried out and his condition monitored. There is no doubt that this communication technique will revolutionize the care of patients in remote parts of the world. At the moment the use of a satellite for this type of problem is very expensive, and it will be some time before we will be able to use this technology in Africa, but it is a picture of things to come which should be included in our long-term planning.

There is still a strong belief among the lay public that in an emergency in the bush an aeroplane is needed. This is sometimes, but not always, the case. If the patient can be safely moved to the nearest medical help by road, it may well be best to wait for the medical staff on the spot to give their report. We have found, for instance, that cases of intestinal obstruction travel very badly by air and there is a high mortality rate. It would be better, when practical, to fly the surgeon to the patient rather than the other way round. Of course, each case has to be judged on its merits and the right decision will depend on many factors.

We have carried out hundreds of emergency evacuations with our fleet of light aircraft, both twin and single engine. They are mainly Cessna aircraft which have stood us in good stead. The single engine aircraft will cover about 145 miles in an hour, and the twin engine about 200 miles. They are fitted with modern navigational aids, and when used for emergencies they carry a full pack of medical equipment including oxygen apparatus, intravenous drips, splints, instruments and drugs. This equipment is kept in the hangar, ready to be loaded into whichever aircraft is going to cover the emergency. These light aircraft are able to land and take off in short distances, depending on altitude and temperature. These factors may make a great deal of difference in a take-off run, and can vary it by 25 per cent. In the middle of a hot day in the East African Highlands this is a consideration not to be ignored.

On the whole the weather is kind to pilots in East Africa for most of the year. However, at the beginning of the rains the storms can be heavy with torrential downpours, thunder and lightning. In July and August low cloud often descends, covering the ground, and visual flying may have to be postponed for a few hours until the clouds burn off with the sun. In the whole history of the Flying Doctor Service it has been rare for an aircraft not to get to its destination even if it may, on occasions, have been delayed by bad weather.

Recently an aircraft of the Flying Doctor Service was called to pick up a man

...........................................

*(Opposite) Imagine a world without cars, roads or telephones. This aerial photograph shows the isolation of a small manyatta in the Maasai plains. The shadow of our aircraft appears below left.*

...........................................

*(Previous page) A vast tract of wilderness in the Great Rift Valley, northern Tanzania, on the southern shores of Lake Natron. This aerial view shows a freshwater river winding through the white soda flats south of the lake. In the background is the active volcano ol doinyo Lengai (Maasai for 'The Mountain of God').*

with a severe chest injury from a buffalo in Maralal, 170 miles north of Nairobi. It was late afternoon when the call came, which meant there was a hurry to get there, in order to be able to take off again before dark. I happened to be flying back from Wajir that afternoon, and the doctor in Maralal was calling on the radio and his transmission could not be picked up in Nairobi. I could hear him and relayed the details of the case to Nairobi. The pilot flying to Maralal found there was a wall of rain and low cloud before he reached Nyeri and despite many attempts he was unable to get through. After a time he reckoned correctly that it would be dark in Maralal before he arrived, and so he had to turn back and land again at Nairobi. I relayed to the doctor what had happened and discussed the case with him. There did not appear to be much hope as the man's chest had been crushed and he was bleeding. Despite transfusions and energetic medical care, the patient died during the night. It is, of course, very probable that he would have died even if we had been able to evacuate him to a surgical centre in Nairobi. This was a sad and disappointing case, one of the few occasions when we have been unable to reach our destination.

Radio was put to a more novel use on another occasion. A man had fallen off a ladder in a mission station in the Northern Frontier District, near the Ethiopian border. The man had a badly fractured skull with a depressed section which needed immediate operation. The doctor of the mission hospital was a good physician but no surgeon, and he was faced with a desperate surgical emergency. He called up on the radio and I happened to be on call. Could he do the operation? How was it done? His voice sounded anxious and nervous on the radio and, I felt, with some cause.

I talked to him as simply as I could taking him step by step through the intricate process of the operation. He would work for a few minutes, and then come back to the radio, and I would instruct him on the next step. This would necessitate him scrubbing up again each time. Over a long hour we worked together in this way, hundreds of miles apart, the reassuring voice on the radio keeping up his resolve.

The operation to lift a fragment of a depressed skull bone is not usually a difficult procedure, unless there are complications such as haemorrhage or damage to the underlying brain or its coverings. In this case I thought it was easiest for the doctor to make what is called a burr hole close to the fracture and then introduce a bone lever through the hole in order to raise the depressed fragment.

At one point after the burr hole had been successfully made with a rather primitive trephine there was a welling up of blood through the hole. This was not surprising, but a little daunting for the doctor. He put a swab in the hole and came back to consult me. By this time he had worked out a system of leaving a nurse to transmit his messages so that he did not have to scrub up repeatedly.

I asked him to suck out the blood and see if it continued to bleed and also to see whether there was any leakage of cerebrospinal fluid. I warned him to be careful with the sucker so as not to damage the brain. At this point the doctor continued to be efficient and calm, and was able to elevate the depressed bone, thereby relieving the pressure within the skull which was the cause of the patient's unconsciousness. However, there was still a constant flow of blood and he was unable to ascertain where it was coming from. He had not seen the brain, and there was no obvious leakage of cerebrosinal fluid. I advised him to put in a small soft pack of gauze and leave it for ten minutes to see if this helped to stop the bleeding. It seemed probable that the bleeding was coming from the fractured bone which had first been depressed by the injury and then elevated back into position. The pack had the desired effect and the bleeding stopped. I recommended that he should watch the area for a few minutes and if there was no more bleeding to replace the plug of bone removed with the trephine and close the wound. We were fortunate in this case that there was no more trouble, the patient slowly became conscious and in a relatively short time he was none the worse for wear.

With such forms of communication, it is possible that Africa will not be doomed to follow the centuries-long progress of other developed countries, for with modern communications the outside world, its ideas and technology intrude daily into the lives of these countries. And such development will be not only speedier but cheaper, for by radio and plane it is possible to spread available skills over a far wider area. An aeroplane can fly direct, thus cutting down mileage; it occupies the minimum amount of travel time for the specially skilled person, and finally it is actually cheaper than ground travel.

Other types of communication are also being used increasingly by AMREF – among them the written word, which is an alien form of communication in Africa. As an African friend once said to me:

*We come from an oral culture, not a visual one. All our history, the stories of our past, were passed down to us by word of mouth. Our old men telling the stories again and again round the fire of an evening, or publicly on great occasions. Most of us, even some high-up government servants, still do not read with great facility. We have never owned books, even when we were at school. There were so few books to go round, the teacher had to write laboriously on the blackboard for us to copy, equally laboriously, into our notebooks. So reading has not, for this generation, become a pastime for pleasure. Now we are busy men and to read a report takes time. So many reports go straight into the bottom drawer, or are given to a junior to read, who understands it even less and so he too puts it in the bottom drawer.*

We laughed together at the thought, for certainly that is the fate of most reports in Africa. Equally, the oral tradition may turn to Africa's advantage, for in the coming age of transmission by radio, television, cinema and tape recorder, this could be the type of communication which will accelerate Africa's development.

The African oral tradition has one great advantage: people develop excellent memories, and can recall incidents much better than most Westerners. We tend to over-burden our memories by trying to take in and retain endless memoranda through our eyes. It is possible that the development of other routes to the memory, and the use of machines to retain information for us, will free our memories to become more, not less, efficient.

At the time when my wife Susan was born in the Congo there was no doctor in the area. The nearest one was stationed seven days' journey away by jungle path and river boat. Susan's parents felt they should make some provision in case of emergency and so a system of drum messages was set up. The sound of the drums echoing through the forest from village to village would ensure that the doctor set out immediately. Happily it was not necessary to put the system to the test, but none the less this was how messages were relayed only a lifetime ago. In the space of one lifetime Africa has moved from jungle drums to satellite telephones, and this advance has brought great changes in its wake.

The modern substitute for these ancient jungle drums has been our radio network, in the first place connecting some twenty-five hospitals with the centre. The installation of this form of communication revolutionized the lives of the bush hospitals. They were not on their own any more, and a government medical assistant or a mission doctor could call on the knowledge and skills of specialists any time of the day. The morale in these hospitals was strengthened immediately, and they were also able to call for supplies or vaccines and arrange for the visits of specialists, or call for an evacuation by air in an emergency. The service now operates a twenty-four hour coverage. At the present time 105 hospitals are on the radio network and besides talking to headquarters they have developed a lively communication system between themselves; the lunch hour is filled with discussion of difficult cases and with the exchange of news concerning staff, supplies and meetings.

The written word, however, has not been neglected and we now have a large printing department. From it are published news sheets, reports, and most important of all, the manuals. These are a series of textbooks for the medical personnel who are isolated in the bush with no source of reference for the problems they have to face, and upon whom falls the responsibility for the health and treatment of a large area. They are simply written and illustrated and now cover many different medical subjects. Translated into different languages, they are being sent all over the world and we print over 200,000 copies a year.

We also use our printing and publishing service to make available the experience we have built up over the years, so that it can reach many countries and peoples throughout the developing world. It is the ripple effect of this knowledge, learnt at the grass roots of rural and peasant societies, that is invaluable to countries struggling to establish a modicum of public health and basic medical services.

Health and medical issues are matters which concern not only doctors and hospitals; they are also of intimate interest to the public themselves. For some years we have been aware of the needs of this wider audience, so we have created a character known as Dr AMREF who broadcasts on Kenya radio and writes a regular column in the local press. Dr AMREF has become a popular figure, answering questions from readers on the medical problems which people face who have little knowledge of patent medicines or the basis of medical science.

These problems range from discussion of sex and fertility matters – by far the most numerous inquiries – to information on controlling malaria, dealing with cataracts, on immunization and the diseases it can control, and on many other subjects of public and private interest. One young correspondent asked Dr AMREF how she could make her eyes sparkle: Dr AMREF replied that he would like to know the answer himself! On another occasion a young man wrote to Dr AMREF asking if he could have his feet made smaller so that he could wear fashionable pointed shoes, for his friends teased him about his large feet. Even the plastic surgery skills of Dr AMREF were defeated by this question. Altogether 'Dr AMREF' is the most popular Thursday night programme on radio, and many

*(Opposite above) A Flying Doctor plane lands on a small bush strip at Shombole in Maasailand for a clinic. Landing on these strips can be hazardous due to the danger of wild and domestic animals straying into the path of the aircraft.*

*(Opposite below) Arriving at a remote mission station often causes excitement and helps to boost the morale of the people working there. A flying doctor, Anne Spoerry, is seen here arriving at Kor in the Kaisut Desert, northern Kenya.*

listeners enjoy his spicy talks; his newspaper column also reaches tens of thousands of readers.

No radio communication, however, is more important than that between ground and air. Headquarters is in constant touch with our fleet of seven aeroplanes, as they fly on various missions round East Africa. Bad weather, strong winds and other information concerning the state of airfields, which is vital to safe flying, is reported over this ground-to-air radio system. The condition of the airstrip is of particular significance in bush flying, for often these bush strips are uncared for and rainstorms can erode sections leaving great runnels across the strip, or footpaths develop, and animals such as antbears dig large holes which could sheer off the nosewheel of an aircraft. Often wild animals may be crossing the strip, or a storm blot out all sign of it on the ground. In all these difficulties to be in touch with the ground not only increases safety, it increases the pilot's confidence.

I have myself been lost on more than one occasion, and unable to find the hospital I was going to; in bad weather, over hundreds of miles of uninterrupted bush this can happen all too easily. I was once lost in the middle of Tanzania trying to find a hospital I had not seen before. Low cloud had made the whole area unfamiliar, the tops of the hills were invisible and we therefore had no skyline to assist us. Fortunately the doctor at the hospital had turned on his radio and heard my call, and with his local knowledge of the hills and terrain around his hospital, was able to guide me in. Since I had Dr Albert Schweitzer's daughter on board I was anxious to appear efficient. Losing our way, and yet being guided in, was even more impressive than a straight run.

On a recent trip to an outlying hospital David and I had just left the airfield when we picked up on the radio a call from one of our own pilots in distress. His undercarriage had apparently jammed in the half-way position and he was unable to land. We circled back and watched the AMREF engineers take off in another plane. They, too, circled round and came in under the aircraft in trouble. Talking to the pilot on the radio all the time, they scrutinized the underside of the plane and the landing gear. I listened in to the conversation between the two pilots. They were flying so close together that at one point Phil Mathews jokingly asked Jim Heatherhayes whether he could hand him a cigarette. Finally they decided the partially locked gear would hold, and the pilot made a safe landing. David and I heaved a sigh of relief and flew on our way, out over the dry plains to the north east.

Communications do, on occasions, fail and it is then that we appreciate their value. A plan gets snarled up, the full story is not told, or a message does not get through. A few years ago we had an urgent call from the East African Railways. A train had been derailed in a remote area of central Tanzania, and many casualties were expected. We were asked by the railway authorities in Nairobi to go at once to help evacuate them. I collected our emergency team, which in those far-off days consisted of myself, a nurse, and Dr Anne Spoerry and her team, and we flew with our medical supplies to Korogwe. We were met there by railway officials and loaded into a self-propelled railway truck which bowled happily down the line. It had taken us an hour and a half to reach Korogwe. It now took us another two hours by rail, for the area was indeed remote and no plane could have landed anywhere near the scene.

I vividly remember our arrival. The engine lay sadly on its side, carriages juntered up against each other were derailed in a horrible confusion of twisted metal and broken timber. Not a soul was in sight. We disembarked and hunted through the debris for signs of human life, but there were none. As we reloaded our carefully packed supplies back into the truck a railway worker, a linesman, appeared from nowhere. We explained who we were and why we had come. He told us that all the injured had been satisfactorily evacuated by road some hours before. 'But,' he added, remembering we were doctors, 'I have a bad headache myself!' I gave him an aspirin, and departed on the long journey home with an ill grace which gave way to laughter as we chugged back up the line. In a press report about the incident it said, 'Hours later the Flying Doctor Service arrived' – a comment which I have still not lived down and which my family like to revive on suitable occasions.

One day I received a telephone call in the late evening begging me to go at once to central Tanzania where a rich Greek gentleman was desperately ill. The message was garbled and inadequate. It was not certain whether the man was suffering from a heart or stomach crisis, so I was asked to bring a physician with me as well. Reluctantly I called up a friend of mine and we met outside the New Stanley Hotel, waiting for an unknown car and driver to pick us up. The sense of mystery seemed to increase as we lay back in the huge American limousine and sped into the night. I half expected to be kidnapped, and the sinister atmosphere was exaggerated by not knowing exactly where or to whom we were going.

We were exhausted, cold and hungry. The roads were so bad we could not sleep, but we drove relentlessly on. A colourless dawn at last crept over the flat

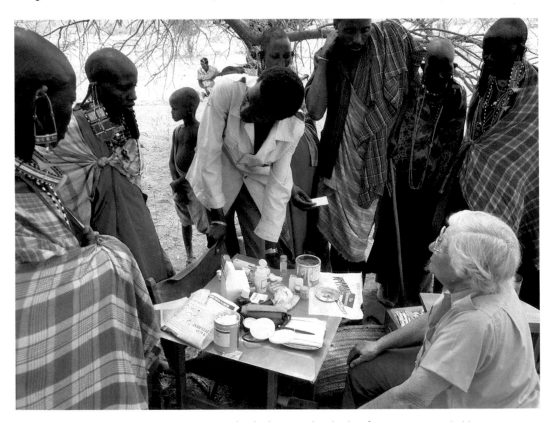

*Anne Spoerry carrying out a bush clinic in the shade of a tree, surrounded by Maasai women. A clinical officer acts as interpreter. The Maasai come on foot from miles around to attend their clinics.*

*Anne Spoerry uses a high frequency radio at Loyangalani mission to communicate with Foundation Control in Nairobi. Loyangalani oasis is situated on the south-east shores of Lake Turkana.*

countryside and at 6 am we drove on to the estate. The track was lined with huge spears of sisal and the plantation spread into the mighty distance on both sides of the road. Half an hour later, stiff with exhaustion and cold, we arrived at a grim looking house, shuttered all round, and still dead asleep.

We battered on the door, already feeling aggrieved that there was no welcome to meet us. After some time a shuffling, bleary-eyed servant opened the door; there was some confused whispering among the half-clad inhabitants of the house and finally we were led in to see the patient.

After the usual greetings I asked him: 'What is the matter with you, what are you complaining of?'

'Well,' he said after a pause, 'I haven't been sleeping very well lately.'

It is experiences such as this that makes us insist that we have a doctor's request before we send out an aircraft on a rescue mission. It can save a great deal of wasted time.

The basis of all communication is the word, whether spoken or written, broadcast or taped. And the vehicle that gives the word meaning is language. In Africa we have many languages with which to contend. In Tanzania for instance there are over 120 tribes, each with their own vernacular language. This has kept that area fragmented and the tribes isolated. Despite this, the transition to modern nationhood has been assisted by the lack of powerful tribal groups contending for political power and the development of Swahili as a lingua franca. In Kenya, where tribes are fewer and linguistically linked, the growth of a lingua franca has been less important. There English performs its function as a useful world language, opening the doors of technology and science and enabling communication with other peoples round the world. In AMREF we have used both Swahili and English in our large training department. Seminars are set up and medical assistants from many different African countries attend them, to keep up to date, and to enjoy the stimulus of discussion about problems which they often have to face alone.

Our mobile teams also teach at the grass roots level, in villages and country communities, where little or no adult education is carried out. Villagers are encouraged to choose one woman and one man, the natural leaders of the community, to become its health workers. We then train them and send them back to improve the health practices of the community. The supply of clean water for drinking is the first problem to be tackled and with the help of our Environmental Health Department, many wells have been dug and assistance in running mechanical water pumps has been given. Village sanitation is another priority and people have been taught to build suitable latrines. The health worker will also deal with maternity and child care and prepare the people for the visit of the Health Centre staff to immunize the children. Lastly the health worker will deal with the most common diseases in the area, such as coughs and colds, malaria, and diarrhoea.

In a special study of the Health Centre at Kibwezi we found that 85 per cent of the people who were prescribed medicines from the Centre did not understand the instructions they were given. Some of them tried one pill and spat it out, some sold the medicine, some took several pills and then threw them away and some took the whole course all in one dose. It is therefore of the first importance to learn the art of communication with the people of these simple rural communities.

We have found, for instance, that people who cannot read do not readily understand pictures: they are not accustomed to translating a two-dimensional picture into three-dimensional comprehension. Nor is perspective generally understood. So new methods of communicating have to be found. Very simple felt pictures often mean more than those giving a three-dimensional impression. These and other teaching aids are being developed all the time by our Health Behaviour Department, whose research workers are seeking ways to adapt African village life to modern medical knowledge without introducing the kind of radical change that upsets a community. My brother, Christopher, now the Director General of AMREF, has been its Director of Training for a number of years; although the doyen of teachers in this field, he commented recently that we should not spend so much time on teaching and training as on the learning process, discovering what makes people want to learn and what makes it possible for them to learn from someone else.

Distance is one of the most powerful factors in bushlife. I have often stood at the top of the Ngong Hills overlooking the huge flow of the Rift Valley as it streams down from the north, isolated volcanoes in its train, to the soda lakes of Magadi and Natron. It is an expanse which dazzles the eye – cliffs, escarpments, sand rivers, arid plains flowing like molten lava down to the low-lying heat-ridden soda lakes to the south. No living thing can be seen from the high hills. Man has not altered this landscape. It has been altered, slowly and relentlessly, by the heat of the sun, the huge storms that break suddenly over the dry land, the hot weather wind, and the cold nights. Yet if you walk on these plains, following some game track that seems to lead somewhere, and then runs out into sand and disappears, you will suddenly come upon a man, or several men, a child with a herd of goats, a woman carrying a huge load of firewood. People live in these vast surroundings, amid these extremes of nature, with distances that take several days to traverse. It is to these people that modern communications will bring a new life and relief from the burden and struggle of their present existence. But no change ever came about without a certain loss. These people may slowly become part of the developing nation, but it will be at the cost of their traditional isolated way of life, which will of necessity be changed. And if they change their way of life, will they be able to survive in their harsh surroundings? Answers are followed by fresh questions.

We are only at the beginning of what might be termed 'the age of communication'. If we could see the vibrations and waves of the present age, circling the earth, they would appear as continuous and dense as a new skin enclosing the planet. From this new state emanate effects both good and bad. On the one hand there is the life-saving effect of communication and its broadening of people's minds; the joy it gives in linking family and friends living great distances apart. Lives are held closer and safer as a result. Records and tapes communicate to us the music of an age long past. Books make available to us the accumulated knowledge of the human race. Set against this is the negative effect of the media, the spread of violence by radio and television and the instant knowledge of disaster. No longer do we have to deal with the calamities of a village, a town, or even a nation. Our minds are bombarded daily, by radio, press and television, with the disasters of the whole world. The number of drug addicts, criminals and the mental casualties of many kinds seems to indicate that we are not yet able to cope with this in our minds.

The age in which we live is making it imperative for us to expand our minds and spirits to encompass the greatly enlarged scene with which we are confronted. In another sense communications have shrunk our world, so that our 'neighbour' is a few thousand miles away, in time a day's journey. Our responsibilities for so many neighbours on such a vast scale seems too much to bear. It is always this sort of challenge which ultimately enlarges the human spirit.

In the age of atomic physics and solar energy the whole universe has assumed the aspect of an interconnected web of relationships. So also in medicine it is not just the treatment of the patient as a dynamic whole which counts, but the communication or relationship between him and his doctor. This necessarily intimate relationship can be the source of the cure, as much as the medicine itself, and it is to human relationships that much of our future thinking must be applied if we are to survive. It is my hope that AMREF will always seek to preserve the respect for human relationships upon which we have striven to build it, and use its deep and close relationships with the people of Africa as the basis for all its new and creative thought.

*An AMREF aircraft flying over the Rift Valley near the Kenya/Tanzania border. The circular patches on the plains below are disused manyattas.*

......................................

Ancient man possessed an acute sense of oneness with his surroundings. He had a natural confidence in his relationship with the plant and animal worlds, which were included in his sense of himself as an individual soul. The science of physics today reiterates this ancient knowledge as it reveals the complex interrelatedness of things throughout the natural world. Communication, which is the basis of relationships, comes like an echo from the old world to assume ever greater importance to us today. From the ancient peoples of Africa there is still much to be handed on, before they are lost to us by contact with the growing points of 'civilization'.

## CHAPTER SIX

# THE LAST BATTLE

·····················································

I t is a busy day in New York. The roar of the traffic pounds the air, making it feel as if one is breathing not only the burnt gas of the cars and buses, but taking in the very noise itself. The buildings tower upwards, reducing the sky to a thin ribbon at the end of the street, tangled with clouds. People rush hither and thither. The blare of a horn like an angry trumpet cuts across the general din. People struggle to reach work on time, or to get back home on time. Time and noise are the elements in which these people live.

Thousands of miles away in East Africa the first hour of the day brings a sleepy toddler out of his hut. He squats and pees in the dust beside a lamb which has nuzzled up against the hut for warmth. The air is musical with the calls of lambs and kids, and the deep bass of the cattle. This manyatta is the home of a family of Maasai and it is waking slowly and gently as the sun rises. The first youths to come tumbling out of the small rounded houses pull aside the thorn trees which have closed the entrance to the circle of huts during the night. There are always two entrances and now the cattle pour out to eat the grass while the dew is fresh on it. The goats and sheep follow, and the herds automatically group themselves ready to be taken to the far grazing fields for the day. The older men, the elders, come slowly out into the sunlight. They discuss the day's concerns, and one of them indicates with his outstretched arm the time of day that he will return. He will point to the position in the sky at which the sun will be; if it is evening he will have his palm downwards, if the sun will still be rising his palm will be upward. The sun is the measure of hours, and the moon will tell them the day of the month. The seasons tell the time of year, and the years, anonymous in their slow rhythm, pass and become the stories of the past. The driven time of the big cities has no meaning here.

The smell of this new morning is not one of gasoline or garbage, but of the dung of cattle and their sharp-scented urine. The earth is close all round one, trodden by bare feet which have long ago lost any sensitivity to its roughness. They are a people at home on the earth and in the wide spaces which are their heritage. Among the legends of the past is one which says that the Maasai are descended from a lost Roman legion, and one can instantly recognize a latent truth in this when you see a group of morani or warriors, walking lightly and gracefully through the bush, their red shukas, tied toga-like, swinging behind them. Their hair will have been grown long and plaited into minute strings which are bound together to form a pigtail. This is plastered with red ochre, as are their bodies, so that they glow with a red gold in the sunlight, a vision of an old and great race.

As the morning grows old, the sun baking the earth under their feet, the youths can be seen taking the great herds to pasture. Whistling to them in a language of their own, high and low, commandingly and soothingly, coaxing the stragglers, and urging on the brown and mottled flow of bodies through the wispy trees and straggly thorn bush. The herds move in a great body. There is not one the same as another. Brown, black, white, cream are mixed like a kaleidoscope in an ever changing pattern. The herders will know every one and who its mother and mother's mother is. They will have their favourites, a brindle or a tortoiseshell, a pure white or one with a heavy head of horns. The dust clouds rise and they are gone.

This precious remnant of earlier man is being threatened by the new Africa growing up on all sides. In modern Africa the big cities start to hum like New York and the other metropolises of the world in this technical age. The efforts to build a modern nation-state begin to impinge on the lives of this ancient race. The Maasai themselves hold tenaciously to their old customs and ways, but in a country where land is scarce the pressure of the new population levels will necessarily be felt by the Maasai, some 300,000 of whom inhabit an area the size of France, which stretches down the centre of Kenya and further south as far as central Tanzania. The culture of the Maasai is founded on a cattle economy. To them cattle are wealth, and previously as grazing areas became exhausted, they would move on and their famous warriors would annex another area for them with their spears. Since colonial times they have been contained in this huge stretch of country known as Maasailand. To the unaccustomed eye it would appear empty, but on closer inspection the grass will be seen in many areas to be overgrazed and eroded, and the encroaching desert threatens from the north.

The Maasai have a complex culture based on age groups. Every seven years they move from one age group to another and finally as elders they hold considerable authority in the tribe. The government has been at pains to eliminate the warrior class, but the Maasai have long known how to ignore such edicts. In the old days the warrior class, who had to protect and often forfeit their lives for the tribe, were pampered and romanticized by the rest of the tribe. They would live in a manyatta of their own with the young girls, and for seven years they would not be expected to do any of the work of the tribe, such as herding cattle, although they would be called in to deal with a marauding lion. The days would pass in sharpening their weapons, practising their battle skills, painting their bodies, and amusing the girls, until some boundary of the tribe was threatened or some new area was needed

.................................................

*(Opposite) A Samburu warrior leans on his spear in a characteristic stance.*
*The Samburu are related to the Maasai and speak the same language (Maa).*
*The black fur cover on his spear tip indicates peace.*

.................................................

*(Previous page) A combination of algae and ferric oxide turns Lake Magadi*
*red, in southern Kenya's Great Rift Valley. This is Maasai country, a dry and*
*dusty land scorched by the relentless sun.*

for their herds. Then they would go into battle; and with their long lines of swaying feather head dresses, their brightly coloured bodies glistening, their wild cries shaking the wind, they would terrify and usually overcome any other tribal resistance. Today such escapades are outside the law, and the young men seeking to prove their manhood have to fall back on the other tradition of killing lions rather than invading the neighbouring territories.

Like the North American Indians, the Maasai are facing an infiltration of new ideas and the pressures of modern Africa are impinging upon their way of life which once seemed so impregnable. Instinctively they know they must keep their vast tracts of land, and cherish their own traditions against the encroachment of more numerous tribes but the increasing weight of overpopulation in various areas is already intruding into Maasailand. The Kipsigis, the Wakamba, the Kisii, the Kikuyu are about to overflow into the lands of the Maasai. The gradual infiltration occurs in many different ways. Those with individual title sometimes sell their land; sometimes there is intermarriage with the surrounding tribes; sometimes there are tribal fights and gradually the Maasai are pushed back. They live on spacious rolling plains, most of which is ranching land, with only limited amounts of surface water; but the higher parts of the land receive adequate rainfall to permit the growing of maize, wheat and other crops. The growing of crops, however, is not part of their culture.

Physical fitness is part of their strength. Milk, which is the most nutritious natural food, is the main ingredient of the daily diet. In their natural state, unaffected by infiltration from the surrounding Coca Cola civilization, their teeth are good and their physique excellent as a result of constant exercise.

They are susceptible to infections such as TB and pneumonia and when treatment is not available, they die more quickly than those with resistance. Their children are particularly susceptible to the diseases of childhood unless vaccinated against them: measles, whooping cough, polio sweep through their villages with dire results, for the children have no resistance to these infections and die quickly from them.

If you enter the traditional Maasai cattle dung hut you will not be able to see anything for no light can penetrate. In the darkness the smoke rises from a small fire of twigs, and the eyes smart and weep. The Maasai are so used to these conditions that they are able to see in this small room and they squat happily by the fire waiting for some broth to heat up. Their main diet is a kind of yoghourt made in a gourd. This becomes semi-solid and does not taste bad, although it can upset an unaccustomed stomach. Since there is no water for human use, like the Turkana, they have had to devise other methods of cleaning things. Sand is used to clean the odd metal pan that they use, and urine is used to wash out the gourds before the fresh milk is put into it. Unable to wash and yet living constantly in smoky or dusty

*(Opposite) Every Maasai boy dreams of the day when he will become a warrior, a stage which normally follows puberty and circumcision and continues until elderhood.*

*(Previous page) Giraffe in the Great Rift Valley, Tanzania, with the active volcano, ol doinyo Lengai, in the background. The Maasai share their land with the wild animals. In this wilderness there is a place for man and beast alike.*

conditions, the Maasai are subject to many eye diseases and there is much blindness in the tribe. This they seem to cope with quite efficiently. My son Mark, who has removed cataracts from many of them finds sometimes that if they have been blind from birth, they do not adapt easily to sight and behave as if they are still blind. It takes time for the brain to adapt to the messages of sight.

There is no disguising the fact that the Maasai live in dirt, but they do so with great dignity. These conditions however do attract flies, and in the Maasai tradition flies represent the ancestors and so it is considered an affront to brush one aside. They swarm in clusters round the eyes of the children and even the adults, and though sometimes one sees an elder with a wildebeest tail for a fly switch, as a matter of custom they accommodate to the flies. With the houses made of dried dung, the floor of the manyatta deep in dung and the cattle themselves attracting flies, there is no chance to escape them. It is a good thing after all that the houses are dark inside for they at least offer some respite.

The women traditionally dress in leather skirts and aprons embroidered with bead patterns which they themselves sew. They wear quantities of bead jewellery embroidered on to leather or threaded on wire. The children wear only a scrap of cotton and suffer greatly from the cold of these high plains. The elders and older men wear a blanket toga-like, and if they survive the rigours of childhood they attain great hardiness from this spartan existence.

Though difficult for a European to understand the deep-rooted attachment of a Maasai to his environment, once glimpsed it is not easily forgotten. Recently we made a family safari deep into Maasailand going south from Kajiado towards the Tanzanian border. The rains had been heavy and on this June morning the grass was high. The whole countryside was green with the red sheen of grass seed waving, rippling over the low hills. The small road was flanked with white mallow flowers, turning their purple eyes to look at us as we passed, like so many spectators at a royal procession who seemed to need our recognition. The blooms spread like white paper over the whole countryside, with here and there the flame of a wild gladiolus.

We were only an hour's drive from Nairobi when the stillness of the bush enfolded us. The whole of the rest of life fell from our shoulders. A go-away bird flew angrily across our path screeching its warning to the surrounding bush. An idle giraffe looked down from his great height, munching a thorn tree and undisturbed by the noise and dust of our passing. A group of Grant's gazelle, copper and gold in the dappled sunshine, continued to feed in the lush grass. Mountains appeared on the skyline, a line of spacious dark trees spread over the banks of a wide sand river. We crossed it on the track, pushing the loaded vehicles in the loose sand. Following the river bank we penetrated the heavy bush and came out in the shade of a great tree, an open space looking up and down the river as it coiled through the blue hills down to the dried-up soda lake of Amboseli.

We set up camp and as the sun sank over a bend in the river the sky filled with fire with bars of indigo and purple cloud. The quietness of the night grew around us. The fire flickered in our faces. Night sounds began. A lone hyena added his cry to the musical crickets and hyrax, cutting through the stillness, making the silence the

*There is a legend that says that the Maasai are descended from a lost Roman legion. This Tanzanian warrior in his red 'shukha' seems a living testament to the legend.*

all-pervading reality. 'This is their heritage,' I thought. 'If this were mine nothing would take me from it, nothing could be a substitute for this.' It gave me an inkling of the way the Maasai held so passionately to their environment and way of life.

There are few examples in history where population pressure has been successfully resisted. Though primitive cultures continue in several parts of the world, it is usually in areas where there is no pressure to take over the land, where the country and climate are inhospitable and there is no great incentive for human greed. Areas of the Amazon Basin, New Guinea, Mongolia, are examples of such places but they are few and far between.

The difficult transition from a cattle economy to a cash economy makes the Maasai vulnerable. While quantity of cattle is more important than quality they will continue to abuse their grazing areas. In a cash economy a crumpled £1 note is worth the same as a pristine new note straight from the treasury. To a Maasai a miserably thin cow is of value as a cow, and therefore a purveyor of wealth, just as much as a fat sleek cow with the markings of a Greek marble frieze. Only when the Maasai accept that cash means as much as a cow, and that a fat cow that brings in more cash is therefore more valuable, will a cash economy take on a new meaning and quality become understood and valued. In present conditions the grass in most parts of Maasailand is grazed down to earth; the people and their cattle survive thus for a few years, then drought kills many of them, both cattle and humans. The Maasai have long accepted and learnt to live with these stringent episodes of drought. After such an interval, when the children suffer most and many die, the grass will recover. The whole countryside becomes lush with it, the cattle wading knee deep in the long grass. The survivors become fertile again, and the slow process of restocking begins until the countryside is once again overgrazed, and the community is left vulnerable to the next dry spell.

Up to the present, schemes to bring in new ranching methods have not thrived, but a change in Maasai cattle management could mean the difference between a slow diminishing of the tribe and a movement forward into a wealth based on cattle, for Maasailand has the potential of an African Texas. Both medical and veterinary science have made some inroads into this vast land to the betterment of the inhabitants and their cattle. But it has been a slow and uphill struggle, and the confidence of the Maasai has to be gained before one can expect these self-sufficient and independent people to alter their ways.

Two nursing sisters working for AMREF, with a well-trained team, have managed to build up this confidence. For twenty years they have slowly won the struggle to be recognized as friends who can be counted on to help rather than to introduce radical change. By persistence and devotion, with energy and optimism, this team have brought about a real change in Maasailand. They are known all over the land and their work respected and valued. They have immunized over 100,000 Maasai children, protecting them from the diseases to which they are so vulnerable.

The members of the team are all Maasai and they each have a special job. Danieli, the driver, one of AMREF's first employees, does a large number of jobs – maintaining the vehicles, finding the way, putting up the camps, and acting as friend and guardian to Sisters Robbie and Rosemary. His vehicles are immaculate and last a very long time, despite the appalling roads and tracks over which he has to drive. Ishmael, the clinical assistant, has worked on the mobile unit since it began, and has long experience of the methods needed for medicine in the bush. A number of helpers go along too, to teach, do laboratory tests and help about the camp.

I have been on several safaris with this well-organized team. During one African winter, when the country lay white as a bone, the grass crackling like hard frost, we set off in two Land Rovers piled to the roof with camp equipment and a saloon car following with personnel. The Land Rovers made good time and when the car in which we were travelling reached the camp site, the kitchen tent was up and the sleeping quarters were already being erected. A mass of ropes and tent pegs lay on the ground under the yellow thorn trees. The light-dappled shade was cool and a small wind raised the dust about our feet.

While the camp grew and the fire was lit, Ishmael set up his clinic in the shade of a great thorn tree whose shadow stretched far and wide giving shade to the parked Land Rovers. Here he put up his table, and the flasks of vaccine and drugs were assembled. Already a crowd of women and children had begun to gather. The women were dressed in embroidered skins, and many necklaces showed their wealth and status as married women, or as young marriageable girls. The children were dressed in a small cotton cloth which was knotted on one shoulder. They waited quietly, half hidden by their mothers' skirts, but all of them staring intently at the preparations which were going on around them. To the Maasai in this area Robbie and Rosemary were old friends, so there was no delay in getting the clinic going. The women and children were familiar with queueing, and were content to wait their turn to see any of the assistants operating the clinic that morning.

I joined Ishmael to give him a hand with the immunizations, but in the end it was he who saw to these, and I who saw many of the children who were sick. I found cases of coughs and colds, and one or two of pneumonia. Here and there I recognized cases of malnutrition. The white powdery look of the skin and the reddish colour in the hair told me of kwashiakor, and I was able to supply the necessary vitamins and instruct the mother in better feeding, but without much hope that the new ideas found acceptance or were even possible to carry out.

The day wore on and the line did not seem to decrease. Fat rebellious babies came and went howling their protest, but looking rounded and healthy. In Africa it is always the weaned child, the three or four year old, who looks skinny and ill cared for. Much of their unhappiness probably stems from cold for they no longer ride on their mother's back or have that close contact with her that kept them warm for the early part of their lives. Tagging along behind her in a tiny cotton toga they look grey with cold on such a winter's day as this. But those who grow up become hardy warriors who are inured to weather and hardship alike. At last the line ended and I gave out the last dose of worm medicine.

Meanwhile the real entertainment of the day was under way at Ishmael's table under the thorn tree, and I moved over to help the two nurses. Clinic days have become a communal event, and the old men and warriors crowded round too, to see and enjoy what was going on. When the long line of children had all had their injections, Ishmael drew the women and children aside and, with felt pictures, he lectured them on child care and hygiene. To them it was as good as a cinema show for these are pictures and subjects which they can understand.

At the same time Robbie and Rosemary were treating the sick among the villagers, and this was as exacting a task as the morning's clinic, for all the coughs and colds, malarias and dysenteries had been brought along for medicine. The Chief arrived, resplendent with ostrich feather ornaments on his head, and complained of a pain in his back. He stayed a long time to watch the proceedings, for it was entertainment, social event and clinic rolled into one.

To get to this remote spot the cars had travelled over many miles of rolling savannah with no road to follow. An occasional track surviving from a previous trip was the only indication that they were travelling in the right direction. These people, who roamed the wide savannah country which stretches right down into southern Tanzania, were completely cut off from the march of civilization, or the development of modern life in the main part of the country. To them this monthly visit was all they knew of such things and their old ways of life were protected by the isolation of their kraals.

When the last group of cheeky young warriors had moved off, and the children, with their herds of goats, had finally stopped staring and made for the manyattas where the cattle were herded inside a thorn hedge for the night, the weary staff settled down by the fire for a drink and to discuss the cases they had seen that day. Robbie produced a bottle of church wine, which revived flagging spirits, and the discussion began, which went on late into the night.

'Do you think that old man, with possible TB, should be taken to hospital?' asked one.

'That child with malaria looked really sick. I think if he hasn't responded to chloroquin by the morning, he should go to hospital too,' said another.

Here and there I was able to give professional advice where diagnosis or treatment were in doubt. We gathered closer to the fire, for the night was cold round our shoulders. The stars began to show, the scent of thorn flower was heavy in the air, mixed with the smoke of the fire. The silence was deep about us. The supper pots were sizzling on the fire, and soon discussion of the day's events gave place to story-telling and we all began to relax and laugh, and prepare our minds for bed.

The tent flaps smacked back behind us as we entered our sleeping quarters and it did not take long for us to be under the blankets. I opened the tent flaps again and fastened them, for to me the great joy of any safari was to lie looking out on the huge luminous stars which swept across the sky, and to listen to the tiny sounds of cricket and hyrax, which accentuated the silence that enfolded us. On this night the distant call of a hyena echoed through the hills, and even far off the grunt of a hunting lion reminded us of how eventful and full of life is the African night. On a level with my ear the sounds of grass being munched indicated the presence of grazing zebra. I felt the immense comfort and companionship of the wild, as I lay on my camp bed looking out between the sides of the tent at the immense sky. I thought of the life of these two nurses, Robbie and Rosemary, who for years have made these journeys into the bush, and week after week have lived their simple and exacting life in this strange solitude which is no solitude amid the demands of the Maasai people, and the remoteness of their surroundings.

Often of an evening they would go off in the Land Rover and visit the local school teacher, or the district officer or medical assistant at some tiny clinic. They understood so well the isolation of the bush, and the sudden joy of human contact and chat about problems and cases. In this way they would get to know the whole area and the people working in it. They considered the encouragement given by their visits to these solitary workers as important as their medical ministrations to the Maasai.

The coldest moment of the day in Africa is always at dawn. I could already hear someone getting the fire going and putting on the kettle for early morning tea, a standard luxury in camp life. I was warm in bed, watching the coming of the light over those colourless dry plains. The air that day was clear and glistening with light.

*Shaven-headed Maasai sit for the final blessing at the end of an Eunoto*
*ceremony during which they have graduated from the warrior stage to elderhood.*

................................................

I stood in the door of the tent and could see the whole massif of Kilimanjaro, the snowcap reaching up into the sky to an unbelievable height, and touched with a rose pink haze. The tea came and I sat drinking in the perfection of the moment as if it was a living thing that I could keep forever. Perhaps I have it still, for I remember it so vividly.

Next came fried eggs and bacon, hot and still sizzling, and the day had begun. We planned to visit a nearby village for there were cases which had failed to come to the clinic on the previous day, and Robbie and Rosemary needed to check up on them. Medical equipment, extra water, hats, jackets, and people were all packed into the Land Rover, and we moved off slowly across country. The grass was white with drought and as high as the mudguards of the car. It was so dry it made a swishing noise like the sea as we passed. The doves began their musical repetitive call, sometimes descending a plaintive minor scale which accentuated the heat and the stillness. Now and then we found a track which appeared to be going in our direction. We would follow it for a while and it would abruptly disappear into a thicket of sansivera. We would back out, and take a bearing of our own, grinding through loose sand here and there, and at last coming out on to an open plain with a large manyatta in the middle of it. The thorn hedge round it was as tall as a man. There were openings, and in front of each lay two thorn trees ready to be pulled into position to close the entrance at night.

The sound of our Land Rover had alerted every child in the vicinity, and they came running out to see what was coming. The women, with babies at their hips, came slowly and shyly, hiding behind each other, and giggling from nervousness if spoken to. Robbie and Rosemary jumped out and began to search through the throng of children for the ones who had not shown up the day before for their injections.

'Where is your eldest son?' Robbie asked of a young woman, who had a clutch of toddlers round her leather skirts.

'He is out with the goats.'

'But yesterday was the day for his second injection. Do you remember he has to have two. One is not enough to protect him. Can you send someone to bring him in?'

'Yes,' the woman answered reluctantly. 'He's not very far.'

When anyone in Africa tells you that someone or something is not very far, you may sit down for an hour or two and enjoy the view, because you can be sure that whatever it is, is miles away by modern standards. So we unpacked a frugal lunch and drank some of the water, and waited. Conversation dragged slowly and petered out and we slept in the shade as morning lapsed into afternoon. As we were considering returning, we saw a small procession approaching, a mixture of goats and children, red dust hanging over them in a cloud.

We all became immediately businesslike, and the vaccines were unpacked together with syringes and all the accoutrements of the clinic. We set up our wares under a tree, and were happy to extricate several of the renegade children from the mêlée. The mothers lined up the runaways, and very soon all of them had received their injections and were wailing in their mothers' arms. The women in their leather skirts and tunics, overlaid with many beaded leather necklaces and long earrings, were obviously of a rich and important sector of the tribe. The older women had shaved heads, and red ochre markings on their face and arms. They made a vivid impression of colour in the colourless dry bush, moving about like brilliant birds under the trees, chivvying and comforting the children, who ran hither and thither in their little cotton cloths.

We were about to climb once again into the Land Rover with all our equipment when a band of warriors strode up. Like the gods come to earth, they were covered in shining red ochre from head to foot. Their handsome pigtails were thick with it, and their legs had been marked with intricate patterns drawn in ash. They wore heavy leather belts with simis stuck in them, and carried spears and shields in a nonchalant fashion, as if they were playthings, not weapons of war. They walked up to us with an elastic grace, a power of movement which spoke of the distances and speed of their travel. We paused as they approached.

'We are thirsty,' they said. 'Have you any water?' We had a little water with us, and this we produced in an enamel mug. They drank deep and asked for more. They finished our meagre supply, explaining that they had been on a lion hunt. They had left their fellows to skin the lion and bring the skin and the fat to the boma, for lion fat is highly prized, and used for chest complaints. One man, they said, the front man, who meets the lion on the end of his spear, had been badly mauled. 'Will you come with us and take him to hospital?' they asked.

It was already late, and in the dark the track would be even more difficult to follow. We hesitated, and as we waited, talking among ourselves, two men came into the circle carrying a third, the victim of the encounter with the lion. He had indeed been mauled, and lost much blood from the rips and scratches in his flesh which were deep and numerous. He was gasping for air, although he did not make any sound or cry from pain. We found an old blanket and laid him on it in the back

*The Maasai seem prone to epileptic fits. This photograph shows a warrior
experiencing such a fit during a ceremony.*

of the Land Rover, while his friends got in on either side of him. We huddled in the front, and slowly and carefully made for our camp, where we unloaded all but the patient and his companions. The driver and a medical assistant accompanied them to the hospital. Before we left again for Nairobi we heard that the warrior had received several pints of blood and many stitches; a quantity of antibiotics had prevented major sepsis from the lion claw wounds, and he had later recovered from his adventure.

The incident seemed to typify the predicament of the young Maasai today. Once a warrior tribe they roamed the great plains of Africa, raiding for cattle or for new territory. Now they are confined within boundaries drawn on a map. The young men in search of heroism and adventure can no longer try their courage and skill in fighting, although the lion's headdress is still reserved for the hero who kills a lion. Like so many of the world's wild and ancient people, today they lead a much diminished existence. Many of them, who obtain an education and see something of the outside world, return to don their blanket and sandals, and live the old life as if nothing had happened to them.

For many years I have lived alongside them with my farm marching with their tribal boundary, and they are troublesome neighbours for cattle rustling is in their blood. I have a son and a son-in-law who today are farming Maasai land, which is rented to them by some dozen or so landlords in blankets, with spears at their sides. From our Western point of view they are tricky and difficult landlords, for they have never had any acquaintance with legal situations and a legal lease on paper is not of much consequence to them and indeed arouses suspicions. They recognize no boundaries, fences are of little importance, ploughed land is good to run the cattle over, and even wheat is good cattle food if you are not caught. These two farms alone pay thousands of pounds in rent every year to the small bomas, who are scattered around them, holding title to hundreds of acres of glade and forest. During the ten years or so that they have been farming in that district, these Maasai manyattas have received enormous sums of money, but not one change or 'improvement' as we might call it, has taken place. When the government think that a self-help scheme to build a school is needed, the landlords are the first to come round to the farmers asking for large sums of money. There is never a suggestion that they should, and could, help themselves. Like other races such as the North American Indians and Eskimos who live under the pressure of another culture, great sums of money are consumed in drink.

Sometimes just as the land has been brought to a perfect tilth, heavy enough so that the wind does not blow the top soil away, and light enough to give the sown seed the right amount of cover, a young Maasai will drive a herd of cattle across it leaving deep hoof marks and a strip of land ready to erode at the first shower of rain. One of the battles of the farmer in Africa is against the constant threat of erosion. The great thunderstorms that announce the onset of the rains break over freshly cultivated land. The seed has not had time to take hold and protect the earth with its roots, and the precious top soil is washed away in a rush of water. Thus the driving of cattle across cultivated land is the most serious thing that could threaten the soil. But the Maasai knows no boundaries in the bush; it is his land, and the quickest way to pasture, is a reasonable excuse.

*In the great open spaces of Maasailand AMREF's mobile unit carries out a bush clinic in the shade of a large acacia.*

This is a perfect example of how two ways of existing side by side conflict, despite basic goodwill and cooperation. The whole of life in Africa is beset with conflict between one way of life and a new culture intruding and altering things. It is at this point of conflict that we need our understanding and respect for the earlier race and its habits, if we are to pass compassion and consideration for one another into the new age.

Another example of customs cutting across our respective civilizations is the Maasai's attitude to gifts. While Western man uses gifts to discharge debts or buy complicity in a deal, the Maasai have a tradition that if you give a person a gift you are bound to him for life, and are bound to give him anything that he may ask of you in the future. This makes of a gift a serious, momentous affair, the full sense of which was long ago lost to us. It may be the reason behind the Maasai's tendency to expect the European to supply any need that crosses his mind – a back-handed compliment perhaps, confirming a relationship of which the European has no conception.

Some time ago I was sitting in my consulting room in Nairobi when an old friend of mine walked in with a Maasai warrior in tow. He was dragging his right leg, the muscles of which were wasted, and his foot was covered in ulcers and sores. He had a big penetrating wound of the thigh which came out beneath his buttock, and was only part healed.

The story was long and dramatic. He was the head moran of a small section of the tribe at Kajiado. His group had had a border dispute with another section of the tribe and the result had ended in a pitched battle. He was the son of the chief and therefore in the forefront of the charge. They had been well outnumbered by their opponents but he led the attack with such ferocity, catching them off their guard, that they had won the day and he was the hero of it. Unfortunately he had been wounded by a spear which went right through his shield and his thigh. It was now a year since the battle and there were all the signs that the sciatic nerve had been severed.

I put him in hospital and operated on him. I found that the sciatic nerve was almost completely severed; it was hanging by a thread which I hoped would make it possible for a suturing of the two ends to heal, and enable his whole nerve to function again. After the operation I lay him on his face with his leg bent at the knee to relieve tension on the nerve. I felt the chances were very small and that it would be a long time, possibly eighteen months before we could be certain of a recovery. New nerve grows at the rate of about one millimetre a day, and I felt worried that he would not be able to sustain the long stay in hospital.

I need not have worried for his fine physique stood him in good stead and he healed remarkably quickly, and with a surprisingly successful result. All his ulcers healed, his muscles began to be restored to normal, and he walked well, even being able to join in the tribal dances, jumping high in the air as is the custom.

It had been arranged that I should fly him back to Kajiado to a welcome ceremony of the tribe, and one in which I was to be made a blood brother of the tribe as thanks for his restoration. I was glad that my old friend was in the back of the plane for he knew a little Maasai and could guide me through the ceremony. Our warrior friend sang all the way at the top of his voice, and left the interior of the plane covered in red ochre.

We descended on the little town of Kajiado, and were taken off to an area in the small hills covered with light thorn bush which surrounded the town. All the morani of the tribe were present, a golden horde standing idly by as we approached.

On our arrival they grouped themselves for the dance. Singing and answering one another they sang the story of the battle, the heroism of my patient, and the great victory that they had won. They have a curious way of grunting assent as the lead singer describes the event, and they move their heads in the manner of a Khori bustard striding across the plains. They threw their spears in the air twisting them so that the blades shimmered and glinted in the sun. The singing and chanting went on for a number of hours until all were exhausted and needed help from the brewed beer which was handy in barrels. My hero was resplendent in a lion's mane headdress, and I could not help a flush of pride to be associated with this man, the material of kings. He presented me with a shield, a spear, and the ebony rungu of tribal authority. I was moved to see that it was his spear from the battle and his shield with the gash in it, the origin of his great wound.

Now a big bull was brought forward and a rope tied round his neck to constrict the arteries. A well-placed arrow was plunged into the dilated vein, the blood spurted high in the air and was then directed into the animal's dewlap. A bowl was brought and I was made to kneel so that the head morani could pour the blood straight into my mouth. I managed somehow to drink it all, the salty warm taste remaining with me for a long time. The ox was then killed, and we were fed with the dried meat which was hung in strips from the trees all around. The morani, who would be feasting for several days, would cut up the ox and feed on that meat at a later date.

The whole skin of a goat containing a thick broth was now brought on and served as soup. It had to my European palate, a vile taste, for it was very bitter and I suspected that as well as blood and herbs the contents of the small intestine had been included which accounted for the taste of bile. This is considered a great delicacy by some tribes.

They then prepared to cover me with red ochre, and a Maasai girl was offered to me shyly and surreptitiously. I have often had to resort to the excuse of having an urgent case to attend to; it has been used to cover up for a variety of occasions, from parking offences to social events I did not want to attend and this seemed the supreme moment to bring out the old excuse. I managed somehow to convince them that I had to rush to hospital, and as gracefully as I could I made for the plane and flew straight to our farm on Kilimanjaro for the reassurance and familiarity of home.

There are several Maasai of influence in the country, but not many. Some have even become professors and reached Cabinet rank. The main bulk of the tribe however cling to the past and to the traditions that made them great in another age. This intelligent and courageous people need to face the realities of Kenya today, and take part in the life of the country more fully before they are relegated to the position of a tourist spectacle, a tribal curiosity, an earner of foreign exchange.

All the problems of the old tribes of Africa come together in the fate of the Maasai. Their proximity to Nairobi and the rising modern Africa, the intrusion of tourist traffic, the influences of the outside world all accentuate these problems. Against these threats to their way of life they are mustering their old arrogance, their confidence in their traditions and their obstinacy in the face of change.

Change will, however, come upon them. The simple fact that their numbers are few and their lands vast, when the larger tribes are land hungry and expanding in all directions, will inevitably make it impossible for the Maasai and the government to withstand such pressures. The land will be whittled away. With the loss of some of their land will come the necessity to live off less and, therefore, to make that land more productive if they are to survive. This will obviously mean a change in ranching methods, which will lead to those great changes in living habits that every community tries to avoid, feeling its very survival threatened. Unlike the Turkana and the desert tribes to the north, the Maasai are already involved beyond recall in the changes of the nation, and their survival depends on their adaptability. An imaginative type of education would assist them. If they could be educated in the best ranching methods which are known today, and made into the Texas of East Africa, princes among the cattle men of Africa, they would regain their status in the developing nation, and would no longer need to protect their way of life, but could bring it forward with them into the new age, adapting it to their new role.

One advantage, which they have over the truly nomadic tribes, is that they do not move so frequently, or so far. Over the years their grazing lands have become more localized and though they may move to winter pastures and back, they do not move all the time with their houses and belongings on the backs of donkeys. Their manyattas have at least a semi-permanent character. One of the advances which would assist the development of the younger generation would be an improvement in their type of dwelling. This is difficult to envisage as, in the areas where they live, there are no great trees out of which timber houses could be built, and stone would need cement and a certain skill to build. At present, building and the maintenance of the dung plaster on the houses is women's work, and to find a material, where at least this part of their tradition could be continued, is difficult. The culling of their cattle would, however, immediately provide the wealth required to make a start at improved dwellings and would enrich the whole countryside, for the grass would benefit from a reduction in stock and the quality of the stock itself would improve.

The outcome of the last battle, the battle with change, will depend not on bravery, nor on cunning and fleetness of foot, nor even on strength and skill with a spear, but on ability to adapt and assimilate new ideas. It will depend greatly on one ability which Africans do seem to lack, and that is the ability to foresee what is coming and be able to take the necessary creative action. That kind of imagination is in short supply, and the ability to look ahead and use the judgement derived from foresight, is seldom found. Indeed it is often regarded as inviting bad luck to look ahead or take action based on such planning. Much will be left to the rigours of the moment. Change versus survival, the old past arrayed against the pushy and impelling demands of the day. No nice neat answer awaits round the corner. Do we even dare to hope?

*A Rendille elder with his goats in northern Kenya. The Rendille are closely related to the Maasai and speak the same language.*

# CHAPTER SEVEN

# A NEW HUMILITY

·················································

The missions in Africa have covered an amazing piece of history, and have survived to become the African church of today. When my wife Susan was born in the heart of the Ituri forest in 1918, her mother and father were raw recruits out from England. Alfred Buxton, my father-in-law, had in fact been in the Congo for two or three years but his wife Edith was a newcomer and for her the jungle and the primitive people among whom she lived were alarmingly unknown. The small white community living around the village of Nala was totally isolated. It was a time when supplies did not arrive because of the war in Europe, and these men and women in their twenties had on their young shoulders the teaching of a village community, the raising of their own children, and the building up of a Christian church. Malaria had no answer but increasing doses of quinine, and the dysenteries took their toll of tiny babies and grown men alike. They needed the strong unquestioning faith which is so characteristic of that era. They were surrounded by witchcraft, which had a strong hold on the community and could be terrifying. The physical dangers too, from antagonistic warlike tribes and wild animals were considerable. Their only source of strength and courage was their faith in their God and their calling, and these stood them in remarkably good stead.

At the time when my father-in-law had come to Africa the whole aspect of missionary life had been evangelistic. When he had been a young man at Cambridge, studying to be a doctor, he had abandoned that career, believing missionary work to be far more important. He was a true sample of his age. The faith and calling which the men and women of that age felt, led them to penetrate the most primitive and unexplored parts of the earth. It gave them strength in the face of hardships, privation, loneliness and even death. If their strength was drawn from their faith, it was also drawn from a complete lack of doubt. They had God's answer to the troubles of the world, and they felt impelled to pass it on.

Edith tells the story of how Alfred would stand up in the large church made mainly of banana leaves, and open on one side to the fresh air. Looking so young, and with an innocence about him which he preserved throughout his life, he would preach to the huge congregation in their language which he had learnt and even committed to writing. They had one burly churchwarden who was a converted cannibal. As the rows of black heads were bowed in prayer he would patrol up and down the aisles. If someone's thoughts happened to wander, and they looked up and around them, he would bang their heads down on the pew and say in an audible voice, 'Pay attention, and don't forget I've eaten better men than you!'

The missionaries of that day knew little or nothing of the peoples among whom they worked. With all the courage in the world they brought to these communities a set of rules concerning right and wrong that were new and strange. Foremost among these was monogamy. Monogamy became the criterion of a Christian man and this struck at the heart of African social patterns. The man with more than one wife was a man of wealth and standing in the community. He was in fact spreading the load of child bearing. In a situation of untreated disease children died often, women became sterile through disease, and the woman's role as cultivator was greatly eased by having a second or even a third pair of hands to help. It is true that in these polygamous families cruel jealousies existed and much unhappiness and misery ensued, but the practice was condemned without due consideration and understanding of the reasons for it and this policy undoubtedly caused hardship.

Men who wanted to be baptized into the Christian faith were made to dispense with wives of long standing and choose only one, which naturally caused much sorrow and the break up of stable families. At the same time the bride price, a custom which acted as a kind of insurance entailing the good behaviour of both parties, was frowned upon; and though initially recognized if fathers were involved, and a price had been paid, these practices gradually gave way to Christian ceremonies. These exerted some power and discipline in producing stable marriages, for the ceremonies were based on a spiritual faith and ethic and the public involvement was strong. At the same time a rift developed in the community between those who were Christian and those who stayed with the old ways. The church's censure was rigid, however, and allowed no room for those on the fringe of the church community, many of whom were ostracized as a result. Clothes also became the outward symbol of the educated Christian man; they were an indication of status, and the man clothed in his leather apron with his bead ornaments and tattoos was considered barbaric and not Christian. The outward signs of Christianity and Western civilization now became more important than respect for an ancient culture which the missionaries did not understand. The acceptance and even imposition of new ideas produced a confused pattern of beliefs, and the old system was largely lost before a new one took its place. This sense of disconnection is felt even today, and many Africans feel their roots in the old ways and yet are confused as they struggle to adapt to the new. The early missionaries made their mistakes, but they did so with the conviction that they were helping those they taught.

When my father-in-law, after starting life in Africa as an evangelist, finally

*(Opposite above) Funeral service of a man who died from malaria at a Catholic mission in central Tanzania. Malaria has reached epidemic proportions in many parts of Africa as a result of an increase in chloroquine-resistant strains.*

*(Opposite below) Burial of the malaria victim at the same mission in central Tanzania.*

*(Previous page) A child leads his blind father to the mission hospital at Loliondo in northern Tanzania. Eye diseases and blindness are common among the Maasai as a result of poor hygiene.*

went on to Ethiopia, he decided not to baptize people into a new church, but to try and enlighten their own church from within. The circumstances and the times were different from when he had started his work, but the beginning of a new attitude could be seen, a new humility and respect for human institutions and an old church established for thousands of years.

I have always wondered what made the young men and women of that day lead such intrepid lives. It was a time of expansion for empire and trade. The new advances of telecommunication (though they seem primitive today), together with

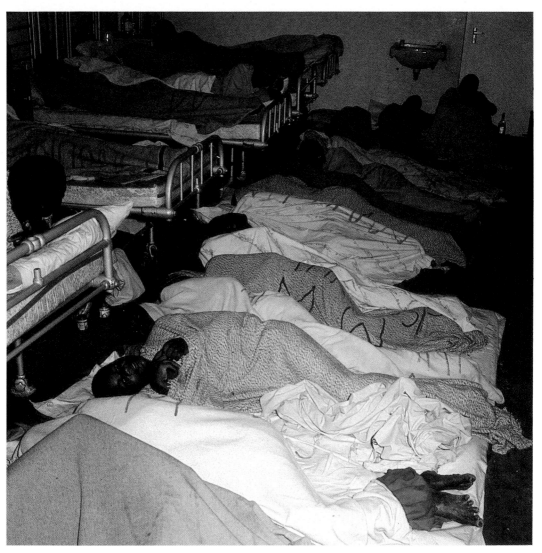

*(Above) A crowded hospital ward at Makiungu Mission in Tanzania. The missions provide 35 per cent of all hospital beds in East Africa and some operate on a 300 per cent occupancy basis.*

*(Previous page) A remote Catholic mission station at Maikona in the Chalbi Desert, north Kenya.*

the development of trade all over the world, made for this great outward movement. As the movement came into contact with other races it fought to dominate, subdue and gain profit. Can it be that the great Christian expansion and evangelism of that day was in part the expiation of an unconscious feeling of guilt, a need to give more to the world than materialism and a questionably better way of living? In weighing these considerations it is the modern African church that must reply, and history that must judge.

It seems extraordinary that even when Susan was a child her parents should have gone to bed listening to the sounds of a cannibal feast in the nearby village with the frantic drumming continuing all night. Yet only sixty years later I am taking off in my plane into a perfect spring morning, the air cool and fresh after a night's rain. I am on my way to visit a modern missionary, possibly one of the last of his kind. The sunlight filters through a thin haze which adds mystery to the familiar scene at the airport as we loaded surgical instruments and our baggage into the plane.

The magic continued as we went through the formalities. Planes were taking off for the Sudan and I conjured up deserts out of the mist; another was off to Mombasa and I could feel the warm humid air and hear the thrum of the Indian Ocean. We ourselves were off to Loliondo, a small mountain town in north-east Tanzania. I was on a routine surgical safari with Ruth Mucumu, a nursing assistant, and David Coulson. Ruth was a petite little Kikuyu with sparkling eyes, which on this early morning were sparkling more than usual as it was her first surgical airborne safari. A well-trained theatre sister, she was ready for anything. On this occasion we were due to visit a Catholic mission hospital, which had been established some twenty years ago by a small energetic Austrian, Herbert Watschinger.

We were soon airborne and flew south west over the expanding township of Langata-Rongai, where cultivation was taking over large areas of the Maasai plains. Out over the edge of the Rift Valley, where the land seemed to flow as if liquid towards the lower levels of the soda lakes, the earth's contours flowed on in great swirls as if huge waves and ripples of surf had become petrified in some antique and gigantic upheaval. Soon Lake Magadi was in sight. Round its northern shores the pools of water were black against the white crystallized soda on its surface. We flew higher to clear the far western escarpment of Nguruman. Shomboli Mountain was visible through the haze on our port side, standing guardian between the twin soda lakes of Magadi and Natron.

Shomboli Mountain had been my rendezvous point on another occasion when I had been staying at Loliondo. Hearing over the radio that a pilot had lost his way – all too easy in those vast spaces where a hilltop lost in cloud can alter the whole look of the terrain – I went up in search of him and made radio contact. Telling him to make for Shomboli mountain, I met up with him there at 7,500 feet and was able to bring him down with me on to the Loliondo airstrip, ten miles due west of the mountain.

Situated in a broad valley on the Loliondo plateau, the long wide strip used to take DC3s many years ago when the British mandate was administering Tanganyika. At 6,500 feet it is often covered with the game of the plains – giraffe, gazelles, wildebeest and zebra – and it is prudent to have a good look first before landing because these animals tend to make a last minute dash across the strip and have caused a number of accidents to aircraft. Taking off into the prevailing easterly wind can also cause problems, since you are running uphill into rising ground and in the

hot afternoons at this altitude there may be difficulty in clearing the ground if you happen to be too heavily loaded.

Taking the same compass bearing again I flew due west of Shomboli and was conscious of the great spaces of Africa stretching away in every direction: mile upon mile of mountain, plain and forest with no roads penetrating their solitude. With no human habitation visible, the landscape had a palpable brooding presence of its own. It is only from the air that one can appreciate the immensity and the untouched space of Africa.

The little town of Loliondo, with its grey tin roofs, lay closely sheltered by a large hill, and beyond it, between Loliondo and the village of Wasso, was the mission hospital. We circled the hospital and soon saw the 'Pope-mobile', a large tough four-wheel drive vehicle, which had been donated to the hospital by the Pope, move out and start towards the air strip.

The welcome at the hospital was, as usual, warm and expansive. We were soon seated round a table, drinking coffee, and hearing about the difficult cases that needed surgery. A visiting Swiss doctor from Endolen, south west of Ngorongoro Crater, had come in for consultations and we discussed his problems before we had finished the coffee. Like all missions, the hospitality and medical interest attracted visitors, and there were other visiting doctors from Switzerland, and others who were working in Moshi. It was not long before we were in the thick of it. I had nine operations on the preliminary list and began to see each one of them, to decide what should be done.

Outside the building, groups of Maasai women and children sat quietly, almost immobile, as if waiting indefinitely was part of their lives. Even the children were quiet and still. European children seem to find it much more difficult to sit still for more than a few minutes, and the patience and quietness of the African children are a great contrast to my own grandchildren! Herds of cattle drifted, lowing, down one side of the large compound, and as they came near the stream at the bottom of a small cliff, they began to run, stirring up dust clouds in their path.

I continued inspecting the patients for operation. To the original nine had been added a man whose chest had been crushed by a buffalo and a man who had been mauled by a lion. Herb Watschinger ushered them in and out of the examination room, explaining to me as they came and went the history of their illness. He was a jovial man, full of humour and good sense and as the builder and founder of the hospital, had all the enthusiasm that such a task needs. With greying hair and a beard, he was seldom without his pipe or a cigarette and would slip easily from German to English or French as the conversation round the table of an evening required. Like many missionary doctors, he was not only a doctor, but had immense experience of the African people and their problems. He could build, see to the plumbing, keep his vehicles moving and mend the electric light. He was an all-round man, as well as an expert, and the mainspring of his accomplishments was his inner faith and his instinct for all aspects of what one might call 'the Africa factor' – the unpredictable things that can go wrong out in the bush. It also gave him the ability to be a human being in relation to his patients and not a kind of white magician, feared as well as respected.

Watschinger seemed to me, as I sat at the door of the little guest room allotted

*The kindly face of a mission nurse near Embu on the eastern slopes of Mount Kenya.*

to me that evening, to typify the modern missionary – expert, experienced and resourceful, a man whose dreams and ambitions had been entirely fulfilled in what he had created in this isolated corner of the African bush. Africa has many examples like him, and his approach presents an interesting contrast to my father-in-law. Fifty years later, we are in a time of uncertainty and change. We have seen western ideas, applied to African situations, bear strange fruit. We have learnt to respect other cultures. We have experienced the great changes of modern science, and perhaps the thing of value which we now offer to Africa is our doubt, and in it a humility which offers communication rather than mere teaching.

The missions have often been accused of producing the misfits who roam the streets of Nairobi and other African cities looking for work; the wide boys and the wise guys who are part of a modern city. There is pathos in the young who acquire some education, and yet find no use for it in the over-populated cities; there is sadness, too, in those who have a certain idea of the new social mores, and yet are not adept enough to use them with assurance, and who hope to get by with bravado or with too rigid and sanctimonious an attitude. Doubtless a number of those who passed through the mission schools and adopted only the outward trappings of their education may well have joined this disaffected section of the community, but now that education is widespread the young with a need to assert themselves form part of any city in the continent.

Long-established missions with years of experience and hard work behind them still make an enormous contribution to the spiritual life of the country. It is interesting that the Northern Frontier District, where missions were refused access under British colonial rule, has preserved its age-old culture. Yet, is survival of an old culture more important than the progress of a people? And does the material progress of a people not destroy the environment and the people themselves? These are deep and unanswerable questions.

My father-in-law spent many years walking in the country around Lake Turkana. One day he was visited in his tent by an old man. His face was grand with age and wrinkles, and he wore nothing but his leather apron and beads. His eyes were wise with the years and intensely human. Alfred and he talked many hours into the late evening in a halting version of his language which Alfred had picked up. The sun began to drop like a golden ball into the surface of the green water. The night wind began to blow, taking with it gusts of sand across the desert. The two men grew silent. Then the old Turkana summed up their thoughts. 'You and I' he said, 'are like two cows, one black and one white, but we belong to the same herd.' The truth of this statement rings down the years and is precious in its expression of human meeting and response.

Of necessity, in the changed scene of today, the missions themselves have changed. The emphasis is no longer predominantly evangelistic but practical. The missions bear a great deal of responsibility for health services both in Tanzania and Kenya. They run an efficient and able health service in areas where government services are not available, and their standard of teaching and curative medicine is one of which they can be proud.

In the educational field also they have set a high standard in the many schools they run throughout the East African countries. Scattered throughout the region in various remote missions are remarkable men and women who live their faith in obscurity. The missions they run are like bulwarks in a community that has lost much of its innate stability. Herbert Watschinger is one of those men.

I walked round the hospital with him after finishing the long operating list. The hospital seemed strung out in a long line down two sides of a square. The wards comprised one side, and the operating theatres, living rooms, guest rooms, in a curious medley, were ranged down the other side. Somewhere near the centre of this row was Watschinger's own room. It was small – no more than twelve by sixteen feet – and in this one room he had lived for twenty years. It comprised his office, bedroom, and private sitting room if he ever used it as such. The walls were hung with Maasai headdresses and examples of their traditional beads and embroidery on leather. A lion's mane headdress was a particular treasure and is nowadays borrowed back by the Maasai on big ceremonial occasions. Books, a writing desk, typewriter and radio comprised the rest of the room. Such simplicity and lack of personal acquisitiveness was touching, until I realized that the hospital was Watschinger's expression of himself, as ordinary persons will express themselves through their home. The whole hospital was Watschinger's home.

We passed behind the main buildings to the medical store. This building had taken several years to complete because of the lack of cement, so the walls were still unplastered. The shelves held all the stores in cardboard cartons marked with their various uses. These medical supplies consisted mainly of samples donated by Austrian doctors who received them and therefore constituted a rather erratic source of supply. It highlighted for me the difficulty of getting supplies of any kind in Tanzania today. The country has no foreign currency, so drugs, materials, and even food, have to be brought in by organizations who have access to foreign currency. The diocese receives containers of such supplies from outside the country and distributes them to the various mission hospitals. But no one could tell how much they would receive, or which necessity would be covered by the next delivery. In

*Herbert Watschinger at Loliondo Mission in Maasailand, northern Tanzania,*
*enjoying a joke with visitors.*

145

*The author radios Foundation Control in Nairobi to seek help in evacuating a seriously burnt patient from Loliondo. Dr Watschinger stands by.*

146

my bathroom was a small sliver of soap, the last of a treasured supply brought in by a visitor months before. The gas heater for the water stood idle since there was no gas. I marvelled that somehow, in spite of these difficulties, there were the medical necessities for me to perform major surgery safely.

The small communal dining room, no bigger than Watschinger's own room, had a long table squeezed into it round which the twelve of us, staff and visitors, gathered that evening. Herbert produced two bottles of excellent wine, which rumour had it, had been brought in as 'intravenous fluid'! We were all glad of the resuscitation after the long day. Herbert's bespectacled eyes glinted with amusement as he showed us a picture staged by one of the AMREF pilots, showing the pilot dead on the ground while Herbert in his hunter's hat and grasping his gun posed with his foot on the dead man's chest. The proof of Herbert's hunting ability was round the walls. There were buffalo horns and the beautiful spears of oryx and impala. My eye was then caught by the photograph of five Maasai youths grouped on a rocky outcrop high above great distances of the Maasai plains. I asked Watschinger who they were.

'They are five boys from our school,' he said. 'The first one has become a prominent government minister, the second has become a priest, the third is also a priest, the fourth is headmaster of a school, and the fifth - the most brilliant of them all — half way through his secondary school career returned to his tribe for the circumcision ceremonies. He became a warrior and enjoyed the life so much he never returned to finish his schooling; finally, he was killed in a cattle raid.'

It is through the schools, then, that the main teaching of the missions is done. There is no petrol available for the priests to take their teaching further afield but through the medium of education, the teaching of the church remains a substantial power in the land. Everywhere the social life of African countries is coming in contact with new values, new thoughts and change, as technical and educational influences take their toll.

The church, Catholic and Lutheran, Anglican and American sect, is a powerful and for the most part beneficial influence, a structure to which people can refer in their bewilderment and loss of direction. But like any institution the church is also a victim of error, bureaucracy and ambition and there are instances where the power of the church is being wrongly used. I heard from several sources of a diocese where episcopal instructions were issued demanding 50 per cent of every church member's salary or income in order, they were told, to pay for the visit of the Vatican Representative to Tanzania. Those who did not respond to this demand were to be refused the rites of marriage and burial, thus making people no longer members of the church community. Although the priest had disagreed with these actions, he had carried them out either under constraint of his vows of obedience, or perhaps through fear of the consequences. I also heard that the local bishop had had three large churches built nearby despite the fact there was one cathedral-like edifice already in the area. Later I saw these empty churches standing with their stained-glass windows looking a little self-conscious on the edge of the Rift Valley escarpment.

One is led, almost inevitably, to comparison between mission services and those administered by government. They work side by side and the government service can boast men and women of many years' service who have gone on working through all the disadvantages of shortages and isolation. There are failures and abuses in both systems, but at the heart of the government service is a sense of the impossible task they have. The unlimited demand, which once sat so heavily on the shoulders of the white man, has become the burden of the black African governments. With the health service budget allowing no more than US$5 per head per year, it is impossible to meet the needs and expectations of the rapidly rising population. This frustration is felt throughout the health services; inadequate pay, lack of supplies and lack of leadership have sapped all resources of morale. As with all sweeping statements, outstanding examples can be quoted to prove the opposite, but these are the exceptions that only prove the rule.

Beyond matters of morale is the fundamental question of motive, for from motive springs the capacity to go beyond mere administration and medical services to make the human contact, and give the extra human touch which creates real care, irrespective of time and cost. To say that this is something which the modern missionary, black and white, supplies is not to make it an exclusive attribute, but to acknowledge its source in this case.

Caring for one's neighbour is built deep in the Christians' expression of their faith, and it is the spring which enables mission staff to give the extra care, and to work long unrecorded hours. In Africa, however, it is difficult to see who or what organization could meet the need. Missions are finding it difficult to recruit personnel and a coexistence of systems is necessary. The field in which government could and will be invaluable is in the sphere of communal health. The production of clean water, adequate drainage, domestic and communal hygiene are areas in which governments can use all their planning and organizing ability. Though planners and those operating from a spiritual basis may often be at loggerheads, both sides need each other and from their mutual respect and cooperation creative action on sounder lines can perhaps be hoped for.

There is another fundamental difference between the mission and government services and that is the matter of payment. In mission hospitals the patients pay a small fee, in government hospitals the service is almost free. It is my opinion that the service paid for is more appreciated and understood than a service given for nothing. Somehow the dignity of the individual is preserved and enhanced by that relationship. However, it is necessary to face the situation as it exists, and it is obvious that the majority of the population could not afford modern medicine any more than the government can. A small fee would help the government, and possibly a state-run insurance scheme might be a more practical approach to coping with those who cannot pay than a free service that barely works.

It is impossible to talk about missions without touching on the notorious competition that grew up between the two churches, Catholic and Protestant, in the last century. At the time the outlook of the two churches was no doubt influenced by the attitudes of the day, and in many instances hospitals and schools were often weapons used to establish a particular faith than the reliable services which they have become. It is one of the most encouraging developments of this age that such division and enmity between two churches has almost completely died out, and Catholic and Protestant are often found on the same governing bodies, working side by side. The most encouraging of all these developments is the new bulk buying which is being developed and organized in Nairobi to cover the needs of all mission hospitals of whatever church or sect they may be. This will greatly improve supplies and their availability and is an excellent example of the new cooperation.

As time progresses big changes can be expected in the organization and structure of the churches and missions themselves. Firstly the missions are no longer what they were. They are no longer organizations of men and women from the outside world, coming into African areas with the ambition to change and convert the local population to an alien, if better, way of life. There exists everywhere a growing African church. Christianity is no longer an alien religion, it is firmly rooted in the life and times of modern Africa. This means that the local church is responsible for all appointments in its area, and a doctor recruited in England or America can prove unacceptable to the local committee and be sent elsewhere. This has added to the difficulties of recruiting staff from overseas as there is no certainty as to where the new recruit might end up. As a result the type of recruit coming to

*This girl was brought into Ndareda Mission hospital in Tanzania suffering from third-degree burns after her elderly husband forced her head into boiling water as a punishment for having refused him. The mission doctor radioed Nairobi and an AMREF surgeon flew down to give her a skin graft.*

149

Africa in recent years has changed. In the old days a mission recruit looked on it as a life work, and he would plan to bring up his family in the country to which he had felt called. This brought about continuity, devotion, a growing of roots and an accumulation of experience, which enabled the missions to accomplish heroic tasks in the often difficult circumstances of the day. Today it is only possible, in most cases, to obtain work permits for a period of two years, and though these can be, and indeed sometimes are renewed such brevity tends to develop a feeling of passage and naturally diminished commitment, with no chance to build up experience. The young who do come to fill these posts are usually enthusiastic and bring with them new skills. But they in their turn have to move on to take their place in their own world before opportunities for a career are closed to them. As in most things in life there is therefore a good and a bad side to this change. The Catholics, with their religious orders which tend to appoint people for life, may suffer less than the Protestants from this 'bird of passage' syndrome.

Most mission hospitals nowadays are church hospitals rather than mission hospitals. They are run by local boards and as a result have lost some efficiency, for most people in Africa including doctors are totally inexperienced in hospital management. Funds still come from abroad in many cases, but the authority is African-based. In Tanzania an experiment has been tried in which government has taken over the hospitals in name, and provides the supplies and training costs while the missions supply and pay the staff. This has proved to be a good experiment as long as supplies could be maintained. Now that they have largely run out, due to economic stringencies, the missions have had to improvise by importing containers of supplies.

Religious expression is perhaps most intense in the Protestant missions. Religion there enters into every aspect of life and nothing is undertaken without previous prayer. There is also still an emphasis on the necessity for the forgiveness of sins, which is in many ways alien to African thought. It is interesting to note however that there is everywhere a knowledge of basic right and wrong and perhaps the Christian confrontation of individual responsibility in these matters is what the African most needs to mature into the new age which faces him.

In Tanzania Maasailand many conversions are happening even today. In one area alone some 2,000 have joined the local church over the last few years. As a tribe the Maasai are particularly prone to fits when in a state of excitement. Usually this is attributed to devil possession, but at the time these conversions took place, the fits were felt to be the result of a state of ecstasy which was so convincing that many other converts followed them and were baptized Christians.

I remember asking my father-in-law long ago if he really felt that Christianity had brought a better life to the primitive communities among which he worked. He replied: 'You have no idea of the change in a man. Those old communities lived in fear – fear of the enmity of their neighbours or families, fear of the witchdoctors bribed perhaps by envious sections of the community, fear of dissatisfied ancestors, fear of the chief and the brutal tribal customs. When they became Christian they experienced new freedom, the greatest freedom of which is freedom from fear.'

The task of the modern missionary is particularly difficult in view of the challenge that institutional religion is facing from all sides today. Ethics and faith imparted in an alien setting produce their own problems, as in any other attempted transfer of culture. Institutional religion is itself being brought into question. As science opens up so much knowledge which is already beyond the scope of the human senses, the life of the spirit becomes more credible and closer to us. But this life cannot be contained within the old rituals of organized religion. Thus doubt and new faith are interwoven together.

It is in this new atmosphere that Mother Teresa's example has caused ripples throughout the world. People can recognize in her life something of great power, which is strangely moving to the human heart. The age-long battle between the St Francis's of this world and organized religion is still present in the missionary world of today. Here again it is possible to see a fusion of opposites producing a fruitful answer, for the example of Mother Teresa is needed to convey reality to spiritual life, just as the discipline of organized religion is a bulwark in a world of new values and insights.

The old African world is disintegrating, particularly in the towns. Though tribal rivalry is still a threat to stable politics, tribes and tribal authority have largely been dissipated, and the large central government machine has not yet taken its place. The old beliefs no longer have the same power to provide a structure for the community. The young move away from the rural areas for education and employment. New ways are learnt, old ways are lost. This violent transitional stage has not yet found its identity and settled down into a pattern of authority and discipline. Against this background therefore the mission communities established round a school, hospital or church are providing a source of reference and of ethical authority in a fluid and dangerous situation. It is their stability and closeness to rural society that make the modern missions, for all their own confusions and faults, something of extraordinary value to modern Africa.

# CHAPTER EIGHT

# FIVE PAST MIDNIGHT

..................................................

If I were to open a window on the past I would see a tall distinguished black man dressed in skins sitting comfortably on a small stool outside his house. The house is round and made of mud plastered on wattle sticks and the roof is made of plaited grass. It is warm and rain proof and over the years the inner walls and underside of the roof have become blackened with smoke, and the acrid tar-like smell pervades everything – house, pots and pans, humans and all.

The house is the centre of a small compound. Other similar houses of obviously lesser importance are built in a circle enclosing an open space in the centre. In these lesser houses are found the old man's senior wife and her offspring. There are houses for two other younger wives and their children, and there is yet another house for the grown children and sheep and goats. There is even a very small house on stilts for the chickens.

This typical family dwelling could be found almost anywhere in Africa, except among the nomadic tribes whose homes follow a different pattern. For agriculturists, however, all over Africa home consisted of several houses grouped together in this fashion, and thus privacy and dignity were preserved.

Open a window on the present day in any African town and the picture is of overcrowding in slum conditions. Open the door of one of these dwellings and you will see a small room with a window blacked out with newspaper to maintain privacy. There is one single bed which is curtained off by a sheet hanging from string and embroidered round the edge by the wife. A stool or two, a rickety table with pots and pans on it, and a charcoal brazier comprise the furniture. The man and woman share the one narrow bed, while the children are rolled in blankets on the floor of the one-room dwelling. The proximity of man and woman makes planning of any kind difficult, and the strange new idea of family planning appears quite hopeless. It is not surprising that very often the man tires of this way of living and as his wife becomes pregnant again, and having no work and too many children to feed, he disappears into the maw of the town to seek another woman and live in less crowded and demanding surroundings. In the towns old customs and tribal traditions do not exert any control over the way people live, and this lack of control added to the overcrowded conditions has aggravated the population situation.

Back at the turn of the century, when the mission hospitals were first established in East Africa, child mortality was running high, and as many as 530 (or

53 per cent) in every thousand children died before the age of five. In the last eighty years this situation has improved and the infant mortality rate is now 80 per thousand live births. The missions are often blamed by cynics for causing the population explosion since, as purveyors of modern medicine, they have been partly instrumental in bringing about this great reduction in the mortality rate.

To the African though children were traditionally a mark of wealth, status, and ultimately of immortality. They were thus extremely important in every community. Children were a source of wealth in more ways than one. When the girls were grown up they would fetch a handsome bride price, and the father of the family could expect many goats and cattle for his daughters to provide for his old age. As tribal customs have broken down the old men no longer get their bride price – which incidentally acted as an insurance, making the young husband value his wife and treat her well, and prevented the young women running away, at least without the knowledge of their fathers. Without the bride price and without an old age pension of any kind the old people are often poorer than at any other time in their lives. Added to this the daughters, having produced several random children in the town and being unable to support them, off-load these children on the grandparents so that their difficulties are increased.

As more children have survived Africans have suddenly felt that this was wealth indeed and, without seeing the consequences of such an increase, have felt it to be a strength to their families, tribes and even the nation. Any suggestion that increased population without increased wealth leads to a poor nation and a falling standard of living has been rejected as a conspiracy of foreigners to keep them poor. Now however, at last, these hard economic facts are beginning to tell, and both President Moi and his Vice-President Kibaki have stated publicly that they do not want to see Kenya families of more than four children. If it is possible to reduce families from the average of eight to the new figure of four, over the next decade or two, it will make the entire difference to Kenya's economy and the wealth of its peoples.

With the fall in infant mortality has also come an increase in life expectancy which has risen from thirty to fifty-five over the century. Some of the increase in population therefore is not a result of the rising birth rate, but of improved longevity. Modern medicine has thus had a great deal to do with population increase everywhere, but it is not the sole cause, for social change has probably had an even greater part to play. In Ethiopia where modern medicine has had little or no effect on population trends the population has still exploded as it has everywhere else.

Social change and improved conditions have produced the biggest single problem confronting African countries today. For most of them it is already too late. The population cannot now be prevented from rising so dramatically over the next ten to twenty years that an equally dramatic fall in the standard of living is bound to ensue. Even with energetic measures to increase agricultural output and the likely input of capital into industry, it will be impossible to provide education, housing, land or jobs for the young who will require these things.

The politicians of today do not seem able to foresee the unrest, the loss of

*(Previous page) Aerial view of Kibera township in Nairobi's southern suburbs. With such high-density housing, space and privacy are virtually non-existent.*

stability, the veritable danger posed by a population, largely of very young people, who are hungry, homeless, unemployed and unable to be absorbed on the land. There has been little or no forward thinking about this problem, until Moi's and Kibaki's recent announcements advocating families of no more than four children. Other African countries, though not yet subject to the same pressure as Kenya, which has the highest birth rate, are heading towards the same problem.

Yet another social reason for the unbridled increase in population is the breakdown in tribal customs, whose restraints acted in the past as a form of birth control. Under tribal law it was customary for a man to avoid making a wife pregnant who was nursing a child at the breast. As children would be breastfed usually for eighteen months and sometimes for as long as three years, this provided for natural spacing of the family. In other tribes certain days, presumably of estimated ovulation, were avoided for intercourse if no more children were required. No doubt there were other effective customs as well, all of which have been eroded by the pressures of modern life.

In Kenya the average woman has eight children. Education is felt to be of the utmost importance and from the time the first child is ready for school, life is a constant struggle to meet increasingly heavy school fees. People go hungry to meet these fees but already the schools are overcrowded and ill-taught. Most of them do not have enough textbooks to go round; as a result, not only do few pupils have a book of their own, many seldom have a chance to refer to a book, let alone acquire proficiency in reading for pleasure.

The government hospitals are likewise overloaded, their medicine being free. One can sit in a queue all day and still not manage to see the doctor. So overstrained is the system that there is no hope of it working for the average man. Rural hospitals are usually out of drugs after the first week in the month, because the demand is already greater than that for which the system is planned. The demand is limitless, but the supply is not.

In the past people have not considered unemployment to be a problem in Africa. Those with a smattering of education could find work in the towns and when unemployed, return to their farms, which could be relied upon to grow enough food for all the family. In recent years land has come under pressure, and been more and more fragmented. The smaller plots no longer feed a family, and a new breed of town dwellers with no land to fall back on and no home which they own in the towns, make up the new and desperate urban poor.

My wife Susan has a small business making ceramic beads. Through this we have come into contact with people living in the small villages around Nairobi. She receives a flow of letters asking for work, and there have been so many people sitting on the doorstep begging for work, that we have had to employ a day guard to explain for us that there is no work available. Many of their letters express with great feeling this new and pressing need for work.

*I kindly ask you to consider me and at least secure me a place for my daily bread. I have been trying to get a job but all in vain. My family is now undergoing a very hard and tough life. I beseech you for your kindness. I will not choose what to do but any job I would do.*

*I have been unemployed for the last three years and the situation I am in is a terrible one. By writing its the only possible way open to me now. What else to do.*

*Life is really sad. I live with my brother-in-law and he only supplies me with food. At night he gives me three sacks and a sheet to use for sleeping. I will work at any salary provided I'm living.*

All who work in Susan's factory are women of the lower income groups. Many of them have six or eight children, and no husband or man in the family who can assume responsibility to provide for it. Some women are lucky and send half the children up country to be looked after by grandparents, but mostly they live on the edge of existence. During the recent drought of 1984 the small supplies of food from home dried up, any little plot of land to which they may have had access along the highways and byways of Nairobi gave no crop at all, and they were destitute indeed. Many of them would often say that they and their children had not eaten for several days. The possibilities for a woman with a large family to find work are remote, especially when she is unskilled, can barely read, and can only sign her name. There is no relief organization to which such people can turn and their need is overwhelming. It is hard to conceive how such families exist. Many turn to prostitution, but at Shs.5/- (25p) a time even this age-old profession will barely feed a family, and more often than not produces another child.

Already the problem is one not just of unemployment, but of a whole generation without the means or hope of earning anything to live on, or having any sort of life. Some 400,000 children leave school every year of which only 60,000 find a job. It is the lack of any possibility of earning a living that extinguishes hope, and in the Third World there is no unemployment benefit to ease matters. There is no way back to the old gracious life of herding cattle and watching the women cultivate the land. The stark realities of the twentieth century are already with these countries, and the thought that in ten years all these problems will be doubled, while the resources will be halved, is a sinister shadow upon the continent.

Take the most pressing problem of all – that of food. If food production were to increase by 2 per cent per year (which it does not) and the population were to continue to increase at the present rate of 4 per cent, the shortfall is obvious. This is what is happening now. As a result it is estimated that by 1988 there will be a famine as bad as that of 1984, even if we have normal rains. Added to this is the intermittent threat of locust invasion from the desert areas. We speak glibly of the 'under-developed countries' or the 'developing world', but none of these countries can develop under such circumstances. Survival will be the all-consuming need.

There have been times when people have said to me; 'Don't you feel guilty as a doctor saving life, when there is already too much of it? Why not let nature take its course? Aren't the droughts and famines nature's answer to overpopulation?' With the human race this has not proved much of a control; the tendency has always been to replace children lost through disease or famine, the resultant stock often being weakened. It is difficult, for example, to estimate the damage done by the recent famines to populations such as those of the Sahel and Ethiopia, for not only will children who have survived these disasters be impaired in health and strength throughout life, but they will almost inevitably suffer brain damage as well. A

*(Previous page) According to statistics the urban populations of Africa will grow from 104 million to 361 million during the next thirteen years. This is a growth of 347 per cent. No human planning so far conceived will be able to deal with such a problem. It will effectively mean the end of development. In Kenya the average woman currently has eight children.*

whole generation of subnormal children – both physically and mentally – are being bred across the continent. The resultant damage to the strength of a nation can hardly be exaggerated.

According to statistics the urban populations of Africa will grow from 104 million to 361 million by the year 2000. This is a growth of 347 per cent. No human planning so far conceived will be able to deal with this. It will mean the end of development, and the introduction on to the scene of the skinny hand of poverty in a new and terrible form.

Poverty in Africa, or any other part of the Third World, has a different meaning from that understood by so many visitors and tourists from outside. We should not assume that because Africans do not have what the developed world has learnt to need, they are poor. They have different needs and a different way of life.

The nomads in good years are relatively well off, as their requirements are small, and their stock produces an income and food for the family. Firewood, grazing, materials for their simple homes, are all around them. There are even sources of water. They have everything they need for a simple rural existence. A man living in a mud hut, with his wives and his children around him, and possessing a few goats, chickens and cows, is not poor; he is a stable individual, living life as he knows it. It is a hard life, but not degraded or without meaning. In the towns this dignity and stability is lost in the search for a living, and a place to live.

Although the rural life of Africa must be improved, to give the rural areas the incentive to sustain the country with the growth of crops, the real centres of poverty are the urban areas. There tribesmen from all over the country are deprived of their traditional livelihood, yet have no means of entering urban life with any dignity or lack of want. For decades African governments, colonial and independent, have struggled with the problem of how to aid rural populations without destroying their way of life. This will be a continuing problem for decades to come, but its solution holds the key to a new wealth. If rural populations could be induced by increased prices and better amenities to grow crops for the nation, and not just for the family or the local community, a new prosperity would result for the towns as well, producing a freedom from reliance on aid which would benefit the nation as a whole.

The towns, however, are a different problem. Consisting of a hotch-potch of tribes, with widely varying levels of wealth, many of them living from hand to mouth in the slums and hovels of the backstreets, they pose a serious threat to any government's stability, unless a suitable policy for their reclamation and useful employment can be found. The answer to this problem is not, as is often assumed, in aid projects, but in the creation of fresh wealth. New wealth comes from the creative activity of individuals and new industrial or agricultural enterprise. Today these sectors of the community are stifled by the ramifications of a poorly run bureaucracy. And until encouragement is given to risk capital and energy on creating new projects, thereby producing employment and new wealth, the economies of these countries cannot hope to expand, or begin to deal with the needs and demands of the day.

This is an area where political needs are sometimes at variance with economic needs, for the presence of the white man creates wealth, but politically is seen as a threat. When the white man or Asian holds jobs for which there are hundreds of African applicants, the resulting pressures are hard to withstand. The politicians find it difficult to look beyond the demand for employment to the fact that the white

man and Asian is probably providing employment and a stable living for several hundreds of people. It is a tightrope which every African government has to walk, as do the minority populations of Africa themselves who, with no political power, find their wealth and lives at risk. They are often compelled to listen to political pronouncements threatening their livelihood and interests and yet have to appreciate that economic needs may work behind the scenes, providing them with more security than it would appear. If African governments can weather these pressures, they will be able to profit from an inbuilt source of wealth.

The expansion of industry, of companies coming from outside and setting up production plants in Africa, is also a source of new wealth. But for industry to flourish supported by foreign capital, stable and profitable conditions are required, and these are not always made possible by the politics of the day. A certain ease of operation is also necessary, and this has been overwhelmed by petty bureaucracy.

It has been shown in the report by the Futures Group that a cut in Kenya's population increase from 4 to 2 per cent would make an immense difference in the years immediately ahead. At present the only governments who have been able to achieve such a reduction in the birth rate have been coercive governments with an ideological background, who are prepared to discipline their populations. No such government exists in Africa today. Nowhere is the machine of government dictatorial enough to insist on the necessary restrictions, although it is to be hoped that Moi's and Kibaki's recent pronouncement will have an effect. With only 20 per cent of the population having access to medical services there can be only limited provision of any kind of family planning. Though this movement is gaining strength, it would require an unprecedented boost to achieve the levels required to make a mark on the situation.

One Sunday not long ago, Susan opened the front door to find a tall gaunt woman standing there. She wore a long frock down to the ground and a cotton handkerchief round her head, the typical dress of Kikuyu women. 'I was going to church,' she said, 'and then I decided to come and see you instead. I am so desperate for work and I heard about your factory. I have eight children and we have not eaten for three days.' Whereupon she cried quietly, trying to smile at the same time; as she grimaced her gums could be seen to have receded, the teeth near to falling out from malnutrition. She had a slight cast in one eye and a visible goitre in her throat.

Susan took her on, and she is now earning £50–£60 a month. This, by unskilled working standards, is quite good pay; the minimum wage for example is £30. Her problems however are by no means over. She pays £25 a term for all the children to go to a government school: the fee covers any number of children from one family.

*(Opposite) It is hard to estimate the damage that famine can do to populations such as those of the Sahel and Ethiopia, for not only will surviving children be impaired in health and strength but many will suffer from brain damage as well. This Afar (Danakil) child in Ethiopia has survived the famine and will hopefully be able to lead a normal life.*

*(Previous page) Nomadic peoples like the Rendille still live where space is in ample supply and in good years are relatively well off. It is a hard life but not degraded or without meaning.*

Recently there has been a levy of £25 per family for new buildings. It states clearly on the notice that this contribution is compulsory, and if anyone fails to pay it the whole family will be sent away from school. On top of this she spends £25–£30 per month on food and £8 on rent. She has debts in the village for food and debts at the factory. This is hardly surprising.

Susan asked her one day where her husband was, and she told the story of how he had deserted her and her month-old baby. He had never paid a penny since towards the children, neither for their food nor their schooling. He had refused to have any of the children to live with him and the new woman he had taken on. He had no work and has now disappeared without trace. When asked why he had left her she said, 'It was because of so many children.'

Perhaps here at last can be glimpsed a controlling factor inbuilt into the population problem. Children brought up in such circumstances know better than anyone else the misery of overpopulation, and will have a natural reluctance to saddle themselves with the same problem. Fortunately, they can in the present day avail themselves of the means to control their families.

To make the problem worse, moreover, we now have to reckon with the basic insecurity in which such families live. This woman lives in one room with eight children. She has no land to which to return in the rural districts. She is therefore

*Traditional African houses usually consisted of several houses grouped together, within which space, privacy and dignity were preserved. Today, however, this picture is rapidly being replaced by one of serious overcrowding.*

dependent upon a landlord who could turn her and her whole family out, if the rent is unpaid, and who is free to raise the rent at any time. She owns nothing that could serve as security for her and her children to fall back on.

We must remember that there is no social welfare in Africa, no unemployment benefit, no help for those on the bread line, no rebates, no allowances for big families or for those without means. This situation would not be so cruel on individual families if the old system of social security – that of land and thereby food – still held in the background. Thirty years ago this system was the great protection against unemployment, hunger and old age. But now, with over-population and fragmentation putting ever greater pressure on the land, even this last prop has been removed.

Strangely enough, a large family sometimes seems better off than a small one, since the older children who are lucky enough to get employment can support the family and help to pay the school fees of the younger members. The extended family is a very real and vital group in African social life – uncles and aunts will help nieces and nephews, and are felt to be as parents to all the children in a family. In many ways the extended family is of great value to the social structure of Africa, often enabling a family to pull itself up by its own boot straps, but the hardship on the wage earner is very heavy indeed. The parents and younger children often go without many things so that the older children can be educated. In return parents will expect to be repaid in old age by financial support, and younger siblings will expect their education to be paid for.

A young man of my acquaintance managed to qualify as a laboratory assistant. He found a job in a secondary school looking after the laboratory earning Shs. 800/– (£40) a month. He received demands from home for school fees for the rest of the family amounting to Shs. 8,000/– (£400). He could not refuse and so borrowed the money from his employers, who deduct the repayment monthly. He is now trying to live on Shs. 60/– (£3) a month. And next year will confront him with the problem all over again.

Population problems are not exclusively problems of growth and statistics. The environment and its resources play a large part in determining the success or hardship of a community. External factors such as war also affect populations, causing movement, displacement and in their train starvation and misery. Populations, not a problem in themselves, can become so when transplanted into strange surroundings. The figures astound and depress one, but the comforting thing about statistics is that their forecasts do not always come true. There is always an unpredictable factor in human behaviour which unexpectedly overcomes super-human odds. It may well do so again, confounding predictions and producing a unique and human answer to this new problem of life.

# CHAPTER NINE

# TURMOIL IN THE SUDD

...........................................................

S udan, the largest country in the largest continent, consists mainly of desert, with a thin population along the muddy stretches of the Nile. In the south as the land rises the country becomes more hospitable and pasture and forest appear. At the time that it was administered as the Anglo-Egyptian Sudan it attracted the flower of the British civil service, and became the showpiece of colonial administration.

During this era I was flying back from the Gabon in AMREF's new twin engined Aztec. We were five on board and the pilot was an ex-Marine Paul Nones, who had immense experience of flying and had brought the Aztec from the USA over the Atlantic and down the eastern side of Africa. We had been to visit Albert Schweitzer, hoping to raise funds for the early operation of AMREF. We had flown to Lambarene via Lulabourg as it was called then, and were now returning via the Sudan. We had spent a day or two in Chad where a sand storm had forced us to return to Fort Lamy for another heat-drenched night. Gladly we had shaken the dust of Chad off our feet that morning and, as Paul had managed to persuade the French to switch on their aerial beacon to guide us across the desert, we set off in high spirits already anticipating the welcoming comforts of home.

On all sides the desert stretched away; here and there a craggy range of mountains broke the monotonous landscape, and a filigree of game paths wound their way across the sand to be suddenly lost in a range of hills or a flat mud pan. After some four or five hours of flying in the heat of the day, flung about by the rising hot air we were thankful to see a smooth strip, wide and long, which was the airstrip of El Geneina in the western desert of Sudan. A small huddle of buildings lay beside the strip, and at some distance the tiny town with its few basic shops lay seemingly without life in its burning surroundings.

As we landed one of the magnetos on one engine of the aeroplane went out and refused to function again. Paul examined it dubiously and finally decided that it would not be safe to cross the remaining desert which separated us from Juba with a non-functioning magneto. After long discussions we agreed that he should fly to Khartoum with the plane and get the magneto repaired, while Susan and I, and our two companions Ralph and Sheila Bowen, would wait at El Geneina for his return. Ralph was a plastic surgeon from America who was on a year's fellowship, working with me in the hospitals of Kenya. So the four of us made plans to settle down in the rest house attached to the airport and wait for Paul's unpredictable return.

The rest house was a relic of the British administration and the men who had greeted our arrival quite casually suddenly reappeared in flowing white robes known as khanzus, with red sashes and white turbans, and prepared to give us lunch. Squawks in the background told us the meal would be chicken, and sure enough after some time of contemplating the sizzling desert, a meal appeared. It consisted of what has latterly become known in our family as 'grenade chicken,' because it looked as if someone has exploded the chicken rather than cut it up. As the day drew on the servants arranged drinking water for us, and prepared the beds in a big dormitory with sheets, and made us as comfortable as was possible.

The sun began to relent and go down below that vast horizon, the soft air of dusk blew up from the far desert, and we began to relax on the verandah which was shut in with fly wire to keep out the mosquitoes.

We went to bed early and passed an uneasy night, for the beds were plain boards which I suspected had been made for the local prison. The heat presided over us, present everywhere, making us sweat uncomfortably through the long night hours till dawn.

Next day we exchanged books and read all morning. By the afternoon we had read every bit of printed matter we had brought with us and I was tempted to try the walk to the town of El Geneina but the unremitting sun discouraged me. We sat and looked at the uninterrupted expanse of sand. Little ghekkos came out and provided us with amusement as they stalked the flies. We developed a game of betting on the ghekkos, guessing which would get the fly, or even betting on the luck of the fly itself. At length another evening intervened; the oil lamps were lit, the day was ended, the dark welcome, and sleep a cure for boredom.

The following day we tried to make a pack of cards out of the blank pieces of paper that someone had brought with them, but this did not prove very successful and it was with a great sigh of relief that the distant drone of the aircraft was heard by about 4 o'clock. I don't think Paul has ever had such a welcome, and the party needed no encouragement to be up early to leave before the heat of the day, in order to make Juba before nightfall.

In this desert outpost we were sorry to leave our Sudanese friends, for these stately gentlemen had kept us supplied with food, soda drinks, drinking water, sheets and even early morning tea. Their dignity and cleanliness, their understanding of European needs had been a comfort to us throughout the time that we were marooned. I could not help wondering how much of their training was a remnant of the British presence in this remote corner of the empire. Something after all had survived.

The following evening we put down in Juba which seemed to us then the height of civilization and its meagre comforts almost like home.

My life as a pilot has taken me flying across the Sudan but I have never gained much ground experience of the country except when running one of AMREF's largest projects which was concerned with the restoration of health services in the

*(Previous page) A Toposa village at Narus in the southern Sudan. The Toposa were displaced from their tribal villages further north by the fighting in the current civil war. Under the protection of the Internatinal Committee of the Red Cross they have rebuilt their villages at Narus.*

southern Sudan. When I first passed through Khartoum in 1949 there was only one tarmac road; the rest of the town's streets were simply dirt-track roads. As you step out of doors the heat hits you physically in the face as if it were a blow lamp playing on you. It is the heat that governs much of life in the Sudan. The Nile, with its grey waters, fast flowing and powerful, is the centre of life. All cultivation is carried out on its banks, and the bulk of the population of northern Sudan live close to the Nile. The north is separated from the south by the Sudd, a vast impenetrable area of high papyrus grass growing from shallow water, the largest swampland in the world. Paths through the Sudd are nonexistent and it has been a formidable physical barrier between north and south for many years, the only connection between the two being the Nile, and the river traffic that plies up and down its muddy waters.

The source of the Sudan's present problems centres on the difference between north and south. First there is a racial difference, uncomplicated by colour, which is as bitter and as deep as any colour problem. This difference moreover is one not only of race but also of religion. The north is mainly populated by people of Arab origin who are Moslem, and the south by those of Bantu or Nilotic races who are Christian or animist pagan. This leads to further incompatibility, and the religious aspects of the war are as bitter as its racial overtones.

After the first civil war, which had lasted some seventeen years and had swept away virtually the whole political and social structure of the south, AMREF decided in 1972 to launch a project to help restore the broken-down health services. At that time the government in the south was reasonably independent and anxious to repair the social services and the structure of the community. AMREF did some research into the feasibility of such a scheme, and the way in which it could become most effective in the shortest space of time. In 1976 USAID gave AMREF the biggest amount of money they had ever given to one project: eleven million dollars was given to cover the work for five years. Latterly as the second civil war has grown in severity, AMREF has taken over the aid schemes of the German non-government organizations and administered these as well.

The hospitals were so dilapidated that there was not one X-ray machine working in the south, and all the hospital machinery had been plundered or broken. There was hardly a motor vehicle which moved, and there were few habitable houses in the villages. AMREF decided that the only way in which a country made bankrupt by war could start again was to use the resources available – that is, the people themselves. A project was organized, founded on the teaching of village health workers: these health workers would be taught to instruct the villagers themselves in preventing disease by adopting new social habits. They would teach the building of wells and latrines, the storage of food, child care and child welfare, and the various other means by which a healthy community can be maintained and less resort needed to the curative medicine of the failing state health services. With the outbreak of the second civil war in 1981, after many months of hardship and danger, AMREF has been forced to withdraw some of its workers, and the stream of refugees out of the Sudan has begun.

In the middle of the turmoil of present-day Africa is a sad, faceless, disinherited band of people – the refugees. They come from all over Africa and have moved huge distances to escape the fate that seemed to threaten them, be it starvation, war or tribal killings. There are now some five million of them scattered over Africa.

Refugees are a special problem, being vulnerable on every side. They flee a catastrophe in their own country, only to find themselves at the mercy of another,

*(Above) A desert rose blooms in the Mogilla range near the Kenya/Sudan border.*

*(Previous page) Wild mountains near the Kenya/Sudan border. Lions, buffalo and kudu still roam these mountains, which remain largely unexplored.*

and victims of the political pitch and toss of the time, completely without power or influence. From being probably independent small farmers, they are suddenly without place or possessions, tentatively dependent on strangers. The hopeless faces one sees in the camps tell of their plight and their feelings as they wait out the endless days.

Refugees are also a problem to the host country. Suddenly vast numbers of homeless, foodless people are congregated on some border. Shelter is needed as well as food and medical supplies. All this costs the host country money and men to administer. Aid organizations help, but it is undoubtedly a drain on the resources of already poor countries. This makes refugees resented and unpopular. Sometimes, among the refugees, medical talent is found, and these men and women can be called upon to help organize a camp and keep conditions hygienic. Obviously it would be beneficial if refugees, who cannot return home, could be absorbed into the community. Perhaps more encouragement should be given to people to return home when conditions become suitable. For those who stay some plans are needed for their assimilation, but in countries with population and unemployment problems this is not easy. In the Sudan in particular, with its harsh terrain and limited supply of good land and water, it is a serious problem.

The Sudan is bordered on the west by Chad whose fierce internal upheavals have caused refugees to pour over the border into Darfur, close to where we waited for our aeroplane's return. On the eastern border refugees from Eritrea and Ethiopia have entered, and a huge camp at Kassala has been established. In the south refugees are even now coming in from war-torn Uganda. Others are leaving to escape the second civil war between north and south Sudan, and are crossing the Kenya border. These homeless people are mainly gathered in camps and the camps themselves then become their home and the problem is extended indefinitely. Kenya has been reluctant to give refugees the chance to come in and settle in camps, on account of its own population problem, but Sudan has had little choice, for the invasion of hungry homeless people has come from all sides. The camps are administered in most cases by the UN High Commission for Refugees (UNHCR) together with the aid organizations, and they provide food, shelter and blankets.

AMREF has helped in the camps by providing inoculations and a team to carry them out. In western Sudan our mobile team, which consisted of Robby and Rosemary, our redoubtable nurses and their trained assistants, went up to Darfur and by training some of the inmates of the camp in the right procedures were able to accomplish prodigious tasks. The funds for this operation were estimated on a three-month programme, but by using the inmates of the camp and with their own experienced organization, Robby and Rosemary inoculated 150,000 people in one month.

AMREF is also indirectly involved with another refugee situation, this time in Somalia. At the request of the Somali government we are administering and staffing a hospital at the old town of Lugh in the corner of Somalia that borders both Ethiopia and Kenya. Lugh town is the centre of the district in which eight refugee camps have been established for over 100,000 refugees from the Ogaden, the Moslem area in the south east of Ethiopia which has been fought over many times. The town is built on an isthmus of land surrounded on three sides by a huge bend in the river. It is an old town of flat-topped houses clustered together, with an untidy market which is the centre of most of the trade in the area.

The hospital is small and the nursing staff is headed by a Tanzanian Matron while the public health work in the town and surrounding district is done by a tiny energetic Japanese nurse. The problems are manifold, as my brother Christopher, who is AMREF's visiting representative, explained to me. 'When supplies come into the camp,' he said, 'they are often found in the market within twenty-four hours. Blankets, food and dried milk are all immediately sold in the town. This is partly because the standard of living in the camps is higher than that of the surrounding population who survive on the meagre livelihood extracted from the desert. It is a hard and hungry life compared to that of the camps, and so abuses arise all the time.'

The integration of the camps into the local community, therefore, is difficult and full of problems. In its most recent programme UNHCR has recommended that aid projects should make provision for refugees to be included in the development plans of the country of asylum. The international community is involved in helping the countries of asylum to do this, although many of them have barely viable economies, and little to spend on their own people, let alone destitute aliens.

There is now a new kind of refugee called a 'Returnee' forming part of a large movement of population back into some countries as the political climate becomes more settled and violence subsides, or as famine conditions abate. 75,000 such returnees swarmed over the Uganda border from camps on the east bank of the Nile in southern Sudan in the middle of 1986; the settlements they had made for themselves had been the target of guerrilla attacks, looting, burning and killing many refugees. Already 63,000 have been repatriated and it is expected that all of them will return in time to Uganda. Returnees do not pose the same problems as refugees, for on returning to their own areas they are quickly assimilated, and only require help on the way. Various organizations have given tools, seed, household equipment and food to start them off. UNHCR are hopeful that 1987 will see a massive repatriation of this huge homeless population with a resulting stability in the many countries of Africa that are affected by their movement.

Recently David and I met with a representative of the SRRA, the welfare wing of rebel forces in the southern Sudan. He was stationed in Nairobi hoping to attract support for the cause there. He turned out to be an old Dinka friend of mine from Juba, a medical doctor, some seven feet tall, who had been Minister of Health there. He was delighted to see us and immediately tried to enlist our help in supplying medical needs and food for a huge refugee camp at Narus, between the town of Kapoetra and the Kenyan border, and for the 25,000 refugees encamped there.

David and I decided to see for ourselves what was going on at the camp. We hired an aeroplane and set off one afternoon from Nairobi. We had planned to stay at the AMREF camp at Lokichoggio where the hydatid research was being carried out, but the MacPhersons were not there, and the house was occupied by a German vet who kept a sparse menage. We had brought a few supplies with us, but they did little to round out the inevitable tins of baked beans.

We found Lokichoggio had become a busy centre for organizations who were trying to help the southern Sudan, or were involved in aiding the camps of displaced peoples. The International Committee of the Red Cross (ICRC) and Médecins Sans Frontières (MSF) are both there. All the aid, and supplies for southern Sudan are

*Sudanese helpers unload aid grain from a Red Cross lorry. These lorries have transported the grain north across the border from Kenya.*

now passing through this frontier which is virtually non-existent: no one quite knows where it is.

Under the protective wing, and flag, of the ICRC we set off to Narus, flanking the western slopes of the Mogila Mountains.

'Do you remember those white stones by a Lugga, a few miles back?' asked our driver. 'I think that was the border.'

Most maps have little value in large remote areas where formalities like international frontiers take second place to traditional tribal boundaries. The Turkana in Kenya and the Toposa in Sudan are old enemies; both tribes are cruel and vindictive and the strife never plays itself out. There is a sort of no man's land between the two areas through which the frontier passes, with the result that the Turkana never go further north than Lokichoggio (except on a raid) and the Toposa never come further south than Narus. Before the establishment of the village camps at Narus, the Toposa's tribal boundary stopped further north at a point between Kapoeta and Narus. The latter was then part of the no man's land, in a place where battles were fought, but no one lived.

We crossed this lifeless strip of desert and saw no humans, no cattle and almost no game. Suddenly round a bend came an SPLA military Land Rover, hurtling along scattering stones in its wake. We pulled over respectfully to one side as it drew up and a guerrilla sergeant got out carrying a loaded Kalashnikov rifle. We need not have worried for the burst of gunfire that followed was not for us, but for a lesser bustard, who continued his dignified passage through the stiff dry grass unharmed and, it seemed, even unmoved.

We came to Narus, some forty miles north of Lokichoggio, and drove into what appeared to be a giant cluster of Toposa villages. The camp was spread over about two square miles of bush, and families were accommodated in conical grass huts made of the long golden dry grass that covered the area. Families had a circle of huts of their own, and the Chief had an extra hut in which to interview people. The families cooked their own food and lived as close to their traditional way of life as was possible. The Toposa are cattle men, tall and handsome with many scarifications on their faces. The absence of cattle and young men was noticeable. Either the cattle had been captured by the SPLA to feed its army or had died of the drought, or they were hidden in the desert with the young men to guard them: no one seemed able or willing to tell us.

I met the MSF doctor, a small anxious Belgian, who had his hands full with sick children of one sort or another. I offered to help him. As the line formed outside his clinic hut I could see Red Cross lorries droning in with their huge loads of maize meal. People ran from all sides to help in the unloading which was organized into giant stacks, with a huge Toposa on top of each stack wielding a stick to control would-be thieves.

A young man was carried into the clinic, who had reached camp the day before. For seven years he had been lying on his back with a severe compound fracture of his leg, which was now suppurating and beyond repair. The lines of pain and

.............................................

*The wife of a Toposa chief stands outside her house, her tiny pigtails indicating*
*her marriage status. Toposa women sometimes extract their lower teeth to make*
*their upper teeth protrude unnaturally, a practice that makes them resemble*
*their beloved cows.*

exhaustion were deep on his face, and as I talked to him he willingly agreed to amputation which was the only answer to his plight. I arranged this over the AMREF radio, together with the treatment of two children who were suffering from cancers of the face, and needed immediate treatment. The MSF doctor told me that the worst incident they had had to deal with had been an epidemic of measles in which 3,000 children had died in one month. Since then the children had been immunized, and it was hoped further epidemics would thus be controlled.

The doctor took me over to the SPLA army camp to see the wells which were supplying both camps. The Chief came with us and as we bumped over the rough ground in a tired old Land Rover, he told me how his grandfather had discovered the springs, which ever since had been one of the springs used by his family when in the area. His grandfather noticed some wild pig scrabbling in the ground. He crept near to watch what they were doing, and found they were digging, and then drinking the water which oozed up from the mud. Since then twenty-foot wells have been dug, but these small springs are quite insufficient for the enormous population which has suddenly appeared. Now people climb down into the wells and scoop up the water with old cigarette tins or whatever comes to hand. This has stirred up the mud and now a black mixture of mud and water is drawn to the surface. Clearly this supply is not going to last much longer.

While I was preoccupied with health problems, David climbed to the top of a nearby hill to see in miniature the life of the camp villages. From that vantage point he could see the women cooking maize meal over a fire of small sticks. They were dressed in skins, and wore many beads which must have been heavy and hot, but which were colourful and ornamental. Around the camp strange sentinels could be seen pointing skywards through the thorn bush. These were termite nests, some of considerable height, which gave an eerie look to the monotonous landscape.

That evening we made friends with Helen Fielding, who was part of a TV crew working for Thames Television. The crew had gone up to Boma to interview Garang, the guerrilla leader, and a faint tinge of anxiety could be seen around her mouth, as we sat drinking beer and restoring the moisture levels that the broiling day had sucked from us. The team were late, and she could not help but be worried about what might have happened in that war-torn country.

Next day we were planning to take off at midday, giving David time to return to Narus for a few hours, while I stayed in Lokichoggio to see the hydatid project. As David returned to the camp a Landcruiser, with several injured people and one dead body, arrived. There had been an accident, the team's second Landcruiser hitting a mine in the road. The vehicle had been thrown some thirty-five yards by the blast, and the British TV producer had been killed. One man's legs were so badly smashed that he had to be left on the roadside; the only hope would be to evacuate him later when another vehicle could be sent to collect him. The others were less seriously injured but suffering from concussion and shock.

Meanwhile in Lokichoggio Helen had had word of the accident, and together we called AMREF on the radio to send planes. During the day the whole party was evacuated, the producer's body lying sadly on the floor of the plane wrapped in a blue sleeping bag. The Red Cross doctor and nurses boarded another Land Rover,

*Toposa woman with two merasmic children in the children's emergency feeding centre at Narus. Malnutrition greatly increases their vulnerability to disease and epidemics.*

179

and made off with all speed across the desert to collect the injured man who had been left behind. David and I boarded our plane and returned to Nairobi shaken by the accidents of war, and the plight of such huge numbers of homeless people.

Because of famine conditions in northern Sudan in 1984, many people left their homes there and became refugees within their own country, travelling to the south and south west. The situation was compounded by near-famine conditions in Darfur where a huge influx of refugees from Chad simultaneously occurred. Meanwhile men parted with their families to look for work, and their dependents were left to die on the roadsides. At the same time the internal food position in the Sudan is being aggravated by the inexorable march of the desert, which every year takes its toll of cultivable land. The population of the country has risen, and disregarding the influx of refugees from outside, the country faces a yearly problem in feeding its peoples. Add to this the dislocation of peoples caused by famine and guerrilla warfare, and the present crisis in the Sudan can be appreciated.

The Sudanese government backed several large schemes in the south which now lie in ruins as a result of the present civil war. Most spectacular of these was the massive (200-mile) Jonglei Canal project designed to direct billions of gallons of water from the Sudd to irrigate the arid lands of the north. Little consideration was apparently given by the government to the long-term ecological effects of diverting such enormous quantities of water in this way. Fortunately perhaps, the present conflict put a stop to the project. The gigantic, multi-million dollar excavator now lies rusting in the heart of the Sudd, joining an impressive list of African white elephants.

A further source of southern irritation was what they regarded as the 'annexation' by the government of their oil resources. This was piped from the south to the Red Sea, to the economic benefit of the north, say the SPLA. The rich deposits were discovered by Chevron Oil, who were recently forced to abandon their rigs as the security situation worsened.

The last straw was the northern government's introduction of Shari'a law, the ancient Islamic law which exacts the cutting off of hands for theft, beheading for adultery, and many other equally fierce punishments totally alien to the nomadic Bantu and Nilotic tribes of the south. Though these tribes in their turn can be equally cruel, the imposition of Islamic law was the final provocation that caused the southerners to revolt.

The war itself does not appear to be waged with much ferocity. The government troops have fortified the towns and remain within them. The guerrillas have not the men, money or the fire power to make dramatic attacks, and therefore surround the towns hoping to starve them out. It will be a long drawn out struggle, draining the strength and resources of both sides, and devastating the countryside.

The Sudan is caught up in a tragedy to which, once again, as elsewhere in the world, partition seems the only answer. Because of the presence of oil, however, it is unlikely that partition could be made to work; rather, the struggle for oil is likely to be a source of further conflict, so that like some Greek tragedy, the drama will have to be played out to the bitter end. The cost in individual lives will be unimaginable.

Among the girls that Susan has employed was a Sudanese refugee. She had a delicate heart-shaped face, and an even gentler smile. Her name was Monica and she spoke good English. She had come to Kenya to get medical treatment for her four-year-old son, who was crippled by polio and had fits. She also had with her a smaller child of about two years. She said that there was no hope of treatment in southern Sudan, so she had hitched a ride down, with no passport and very little money.

Once in Nairobi she had taken up with a Kikuyu man who had given her two more children, and for several years she had lived in a village on the outskirts of Nairobi. One day she was picked up by the police, and sentenced to three months in gaol for transgressing the immigration laws. Susan went down to the gaol and managed to get her released on condition that she left the country within a month. All attempts to get her Kikuyu friend to marry her failed; further attempts to register her as a Kenyan or a refugee also met with no success. To be a refugee it is necessary to prove political persecution as a reason for moving. The day approached and finally all that could be done was to put her on a lorry bound for Juba, with enough money for the journey and food on the way. She and her four little offspring, the crippled one riding high up on the lorry, were ready for the long journey home. Monica flashed her sad smile as they left. Within six months the war in the south had flared up again and back came Monica with the whole family.

'They are starving us out,' she said. 'We have nothing to eat and so I came back. The Sudanese Embassy is helping me.' Since then she has disappeared. How many times could Monica's case be multiplied?

As I fly back to Kenya from Europe, with the first light that creeps in under the blinds of the aeroplane, I see the expanse of the Sudan. Its blue distances, even from 35,000 feet, stretch to the horizon on either side of the plane, and in the east the orange glow of dawn is already hot and flaming, as its master the sun comes up to rule another day – a cruelly hot day in which one cannot imagine any immediate answers being forthcoming. Perhaps like many other parts of Africa, the solutions lie in the slow march of history and time.

*The Toposa build their huts with long, golden dry grass, like their neighbours the Dinka. This hut is the Red Cross surgery.*

# CHAPTER TEN

# NATURE'S REVENGE

.......................................

One cannot speak of Africa nowadays without raising in many people's minds the image of Ethiopia and of the gigantic efforts made by the western world to aid that country in its recent unprecedented famine.

Ethiopia is a country of high mountains and gorges, like that of the Colorado Canyons, with ridge after ridge of flat-topped mountains and precipices, a country of fierce men and medieval institutions, of a church which traces its history back to Athanasius, the first Bishop of Alexandria in A D 328. It is a country of extremes and contrasts, caught between barbarity and ancient traditions, with a wild history full of violence and assassinations.

Against this background the late Emperor Haile Selassie kept a court of medieval splendour coupled with a Victorian formality and elegance. His palace was furnished by Waring & Gillow, and he kept two lions at the door. His throne was golden and ornately decorated. It was constructed strangely high off the ground, for his predecessor was a tall man. Rumour has it that his assassination was arranged by Haile Selassie who subsequently succeeded him as Emperor. Haile Selassie was very short, with hands and feet as delicate as a ballet dancer. He had a particular servant who travelled with him throughout the world, who was the guardian of fifty cushions which he would slip judiciously beneath the imperial feet to prevent them from dangling ridiculously before visiting delegations. He preferred to interview people from behind a desk, where his diminutive height could not be observed. I was able to see these things at first hand, for these were the exact circumstances in which Susan and I met the Emperor during a visit we paid to Addis in the early 1950s.

We had flown up to visit some of the places where Susan's father had worked twenty years before. As we looked down upon the northern deserts of Kenya and the bare lava mountains of southern Ethiopia, we thought of the safari he had done covering that barren and wild area on foot, with a few mules to carry his possessions. Alfred Buxton had become a great personal friend of the Emperor and when the Italians overran Addis in 1936, the Emperor, as he was about to go into exile, called Alfred to his palace. He asked him to take care of a priceless Bible, the first to be translated from the ancient Geez language – the priestly language then still used in the churches – into modern Amharic. This task had been carried out by the old monks in the monasteries, at the instigation of the Emperor, encouraged by Alfred. Written out laboriously by hand on parchment the great volume weighed a ton, and was as priceless as gold.

Susan's father took it, and managed to get it to England where he collected the money to have the New Testament copied and printed. These copies found their way back to the monasteries, and perhaps they are even now a source of comfort and courage in the dire circumstances of the church in Ethiopia today. The original in parchment returned safely with the Emperor to Ethiopia when he went back to his country from exile. It is now lost to history, and its fate seems to reflect the fate of the copper plates that had reproduced the New Testament in England, for the night that Alfred was killed in the blitz on London, Guildford was also bombed and the printing works and the plates were destroyed.

These were the events which lay behind our wish to visit Addis and the northern town of Gondar where another mission station had been established. Alfred's work had had a particular aim: that of bringing new life to the church through translating the Bible into a known language, rather than trying to convert the old Christians from their established ways. He had had a large mission compound in Addis, which at the time was particularly sensitive to the intrusion of foreigners, and there he worked quietly through Ethiopians and saw the flowering of a new spiritual life in the church. It was a dramatic occasion when his Ethiopian leader, a tall handsome Amhara of great dignity and power, stood up in the old round cathedral and read the lesson in Amharic, the language of the people, for the first time in over a thousand years. The stunned silence which followed spoke eloquently of the surprise and joy of the people.

On the day we visited the Emperor he was living in the little Gedi or Palace. We nervously circumnavigated the lions, who looked moth-eaten and sickly. They were chained and did not take any notice of us although their presence on the doorstep was meant to test the courage of would-be visitors. We were met and ushered into a large hall to wait. After a considerable pause, in which we were able to take note of the marble pillars and velvet furnishings, we were called into the Emperor's presence. We had been carefully coached about how to behave, how to bow and advance, how to bow again and leave walking backwards. We were also told not to speak first but to wait to be addressed.

We found ourselves sitting opposite a tiny, but dignified figure. The Emperor had a halo of black hair, as in all Ethiopian pictures, and deep set eyes which looked at us curiously. He said nothing and the silence became heavy; we felt lost and did not know how to carry on.

Finally, breaking all the rules Susan said: 'Your Imperial Majesty, do you

*(Opposite above) Ethiopian village scene in the mountains near Dessie at dawn. Two figures sit huddled in their blankets to protect them from the morning chill.*

*(Opposite below) Highland scene near Gonder in Ethiopia. It is essential that more emphasis be placed on encouraging the peasant farmer in Africa to produce more.*

*(Previous page) 'The times are so strange that though the sun is far away it comes through the cloud and burns everything up. The earth is not growing things as usual, but is turning to dust under our feet and disappearing. There is no worse time than now'—Bishop of Lasta, January 1985. A highland valley in Walo province.*

remember my father?'

And after a pause the Emperor replied; 'How could I ever forget him?'

Haile Selassie was an autocrat surrounded by a court who bowed and scraped as to some legendary potentate. His rule, however, did not extend much beyond the confines of Addis. The rest of that huge country was ruled by Ras's, who were like minor kings under his imperial sway. He encouraged students to go abroad, because educational facilities were limited in Addis, but on their return, full of new ideas and modern know-how, he suppressed them ruthlessly, and thus contributed to the resentment that led to the revolution.

Haile Selassie's downfall derived ultimately from his failure to grasp and deal with the land tenure problem. The land was held feudally by the powerful church, and the Ras's and minor barons. The peasants were kept in subservient poverty by this system, for each peasant had to pay a disproportionate amount of his meagre harvest to his landlord. The oppressive situation was exacerbated by the famines in Tigre in the north in 1969 and 1974 and the Emperor did little or nothing to relieve the starvation, which contributed further to his unpopularity. Some two million people are thought to have died. It was rumoured at the time that Tigre province had been rebellious to the Emperor's rule and that this was why he did so little to help them in their need. Latterly he and his court became decadent and corrupt, which added fuel to the fire.

Famines have been a regular occurrence in Ethiopia for hundreds of years. The grisly sight of starvation and hunger has become familiar, and therefore no longer astonishing. Mengistu's government appears to have been no more concerned than Haile Selassie's over the recent famine, and did little to alleviate it. It has however made a crude attempt to move population from the north to the south – possibly for political rather than humanitarian reasons. Although basically a sound plan it was badly administered: people were compelled to move from the north and from the camps to areas where no preparation at all had been made for them, so that they suffered great hardship. If they survive it is possible that the south will prove a much better agricultural proposition for them than the famine-ravished altitudes of the north, for it is fertile and relatively uninhabited.

In 1974 when foreign agencies went to the aid of the starving areas, they dropped food on the villages. As a result there was no major movement of population and the inhabitants were on the land ready to replant immediately the rain fell. In 1985 not only were there huge movements of population into the camps but all the seed for replanting had been consumed as a last resort.

The methods of land cultivation and tillage are said to stem from Roman times. These archaic methods result in land destruction and deforestation. At the same time the population, as in other parts of Africa, has doubled during the last twenty years, and the land can no longer sustain it in the devastated northern areas.

The staple food of Ethiopians is a grain called tef. The government now controls the whole crop, but offers such a low price that the peasants do not trouble to grow more than a subsistence crop on land which could produce enough to feed a proportion of this increased population. This is a common occurrence in Africa and

*Priest holding an old parchment bible in the twelfth-century rock church at Lalibela. This bible is written in Geez, ancient language of the church, from which the present-day language of Amharic is derived.*

is one of the main reasons for the fall in food production per head. Without an incentive peasant farmers will produce little or no surplus. People are encouraged however to grow wheat because it earns foreign currency.

David visited some of the famine camps and described them to me. I quote from his writing.

*Each morning in Lalibela the people come down from the mountainside to the World Vision Camp to be fed. Those who have cards are eligible for feeding and they sit in long lines of thousands for hours and hours just waiting to be fed.*

*Those who have not yet received cards, the newcomers, line up alongside, hoping to be 'accepted'. Dr Peter Jordans, the resident doctor from Holland, screens this group as fairly as possible. It is tragic to watch the selection, the camp can only feed so many people and many of the starving have to be left out. 'What else can you do?' Those who are refused retire in a dignified manner up the bare mountainside, to return the following day until their emaciation gains them access to the camp.*

*For many the only form of food in this community of displaced persons was the grass seeds beneath the soil. We found isolated mothers with their children in open ground, scratching the earth looking for seeds and, as they scratched, the soil blew away in the wind. We walked up to one of them and he held up a handful of seeds for us to see. This was the product of a day's scratching. Starting at dawn these people scratch until the sun goes down when their hands get numbed by the cold, for the altitude is as much as 12,000 feet in some areas.*

*Not far from these people we came across a young child lying alone in a heap on the ground. She was sobbing to herself, and nobody was nearby or interested in her plight. She told us that her parents had both died two days ago, and today her last sister had died. Now she was alone, aged five, with nowhere to go and nobody to be with. She literally didn't know which way to turn.*

*Here, where everyone hangs on the brink of starvation, it is all they can do to look after themselves. Times are so hard that each mother fights to look after her own children. To take on others would be to jeopardize their own lives. Orphans are reluctantly left to face the elements and fend for themselves.*

David's descriptions speak for themselves. According to some sources, well over a million people died during the famine yet the Ethiopian highlander preserves a dignified independence and acceptance of his lot. Despite the need for selection for entry to the camps there was no arguing or fighting; those who were refused withdrew quietly to the bitter cold of the mountainside. Inwardly they were strengthened by their faith. It was the time of Timket when the church held a carnival, and celebrations took place to commemorate the baptism of Christ in the River Jordan. For them it was the moment when 'Christ took on flesh' and somehow this sense of a deity sharing in their misery sustained them.

The church in Ethiopia is the old Coptic church whose traditions are basically Christian, though overlaid with legend and superstition, and underpinned with rituals which go back to 1000 BC – the age of Solomon, from whom the royal house of Ethiopia is said to descend. Tradition has it that the Queen of Sheba came from Ethiopia and that when visiting Solomon's court with her rich train of attendants she

*A boy brings his young brother into a relief camp at Lalibela. The sick child can no longer see but the camp doctor is later able to save his life and sight.*

*Famine victims camp out on the mountainside at Lalibela in the Ethiopian highlands. Many have come great distances through the mountains to the relief camps only to find that there is insufficient food for everyone. Living off grass seed, they wait and hope.*

......................................

became pregnant with his child; whereupon she returned to her own country and with this child established the royal dynasty. The Christian-based Coptic church is found mainly in the north and north west of the country, and also has great churches in Addis Ababa. The south and south east of the country is mainly Moslem, while Falasha Jews are settled in the west.

Until the present day the Coptic church has been both rich and powerful and has owned enormous forests and tracts of land. Since being taken over by government and people, these forests have been mercilessly pillaged. As you fly into Addis, where the mountain slopes were once covered with thick and noble woodland, you now see a bare mountainside covered with the amputated stumps of great trees. Although tree planting is encouraged through peasant associations, the planting is not supervised, so that the trees quickly die and the enterprise is abandoned.

Today the church is being stripped of its wealth. Few young people are entering the monasteries and some priests are even being forced to sell their sacred relics. The government is committed to the eradication of all religion, and the old Christian church in the north is experiencing a time of great stringency and persecution. The people however are still devout and much of their life is centred round the church.

David was present at one of the twelfth-century rock-hewn churches of Lalibela for the celebration of Timket. The priests gathered in the courtyard of Beta Maryam (Church of Mary) in the early morning. Robed in velvet and silk they carried beautiful processional crosses and clouds of incense vapour rose from their bronze burners, filling the air. On their heads they bore the holy tabots (tablets of gold, wood and stone engraved with the Ten Commandments) concealed from the layman's eyes by silk brocades. These tabots are only brought out once a year for this ceremony and no one but a priest is allowed to see or touch them. It was a scene full of colour and splendour, a spectacle of glorious pageantry. Yet on closer inspection it became clear that all this beautiful religious paraphernalia was centuries old and the priests' robes and colourful embroidered umbrellas were threadbare and torn. In this time of hardship the church was only just surviving and had no money to restore or maintain its ceremonial regalia. As the priests left the church for the long march down the hillside, carrying the tabots to a special tented church on the edge of the town, they stopped to bless the pilgrims and famine victims who had struggled to be present. Kissing their hand crosses they touched these people's foreheads and hands. The scene was warm with humanity, and with the defiance of the spirit against the fearful odds of the mountainside and camps outside. The chants rose and fell, as the spiritual roots of the people were refreshed.

From David's reports it would seem that the ancient church of Ethiopia is undergoing the kind of persecution that the Orthodox church in Russia has experienced during the last sixty or so years. The Bishop of Lasta spoke as if he thought it would be the last time that the celebrations, which reached back some eight hundred years, would be allowed to be held. Addressing the congregation in his glittering robes and mitre, he said: 'The times are so strange, that though the sun is far away it comes through the cloud and burns everything up. The earth is not growing things as usual, but is turning to dust under our feet and disappearing. There is no worse time than now.'

There is an inscription on an old Crusader's tomb which reads: 'He did the best things in the worst times, and hoped them in the impossible.' So the worst times lead us to think of hope and where it can be found out of such circumstances. Certainly aid from outside has given hope and relief and has had its successes. It has also uncovered problems which pertain wherever aid is used in Africa.

The first two decades of aid to the Third World, and in particular Africa, have been largely a failure. The projects, started with such enthusiasm, have petered out and are no longer operative a few years later. Huge sums for relief all over the continent have not been used for the ends for which they were given. Even food has been syphoned off and sold for profit. Technology was introduced where there was no hope of maintenance or practical application. Little now remains to show for so much cost and labour.

One of the most important lessons that we have learnt is that it is useless to set up a project where local participation and commitment is absent. To secure this requires lengthy groundwork. Until the people understand what is proposed, and share in the decision to start the project, and make their commitment by contributing something towards its completion and maintenance, there is little hope that it will survive the presence and enthusiasm of its instigators. Local participation leading to commitment is therefore the first requirement for any successful aid project.

It has to be squarely faced that aid is subject to widespread corruption. It is essential therefore for aid donors to insist on the supervision of distribution of money or goods by one of their own nationals or members. Proper supervision of this kind is the second necessity for successful aid, and this is more and more

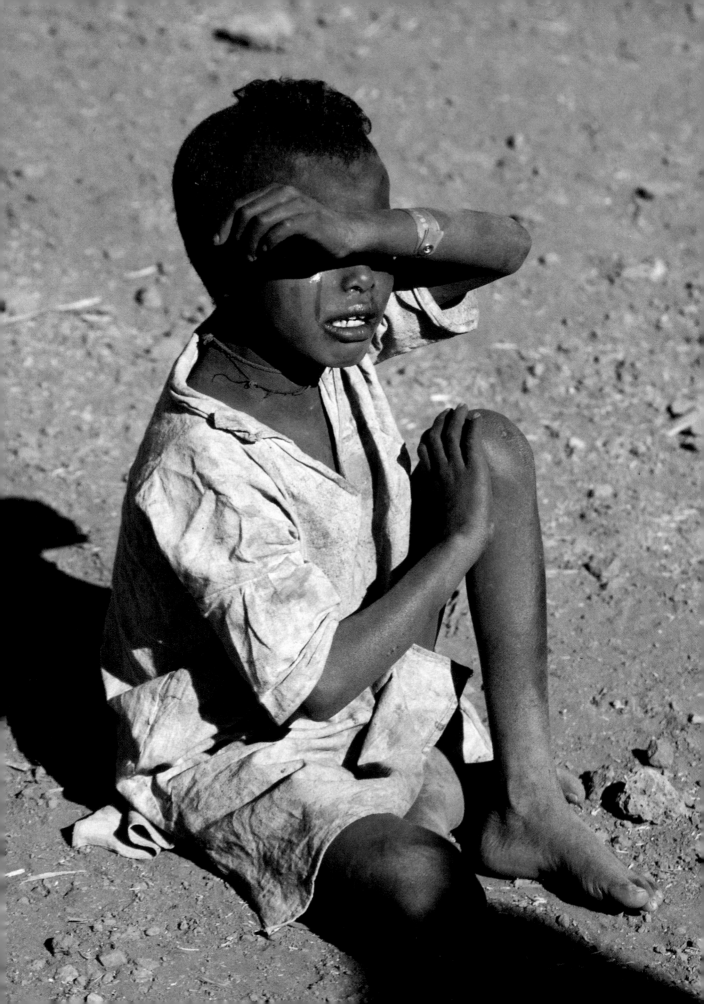

recognized by the charitable organizations involved. The money is, after all, taxpayers' money and the Western donors are disenchanted with aid because of its abuses.

Projects are mostly funded for two or three, or even five, years at a time. In AMREF our experience has been that most projects need funding for ten to fifteen years, if they are to last and become a genuine established feature in the community. The protracted period of time required for anything real to grow has to be recognized by those wishing to help Africa. In their initial stages projects need considerable time to recruit staff, bring equipment to the site, deal with the inevitable bureaucratic details of permits, get to know the people, find accommodation and dispose of hundreds of other chores. Inevitably false starts are made. Priorities have to be rethought in the light of experience and the project adjusted accordingly. By the third year the project should be well underway and the training of counterparts can begin. Gradually the local population begins to get used to the project and to accept it as part of the social scene. But all this takes time.

In many instances aid has been given for advanced technology, especially in the medical field, which has proved unsuitable and of limited use, or cannot be maintained after installation. With the tiny budget that the Ministry of Health has to use on the health of a whole nation (often no more than US$3 per head of population per year) it is criminal to instal heart machines in a hospital, spending thousands of pounds to help a very few. This kind of thinking has brought about many disasters and much waste.

One notable example occurred in Kenya at the time of independence. To celebrate the occasion a large company in Nairobi decided to donate an 'Independence' present to the El Molo tribe on the shores of Lake Turkana. They thought that a fishing boat would be suitable as this tribe is dependent on fish caught from the lake for its staple diet. They had a fibreglass boat built and taken from Nairobi at great trouble and cost up the long and rough road to Loyengelani on the eastern shore of the lake. The difficult task was finally accomplished and this beautiful boat arrived. On the day of the presentation a government minister flew up with the senior directors of the company. There was a good collection of visitors as well as the whole El Molo tribe present to meet them. The formal speeches were made by the Minister and the donors, and the boat was duly handed over. The company was about to move thankfully out of the sun, and have a quick gin and tonic before lunch, when the Chief of the El Molo asked whether he might make a speech of thanks. Rather reluctantly the VIPs stood a little longer in the sun and listened to the Chief. The gist of what he said was as follows. 'I would like to thank the visitors today for coming and presenting us with this fine boat, but in fact my people already know how to fish and we do so by spearing the fish from our wooden rafts, and this we do rather successfully. Would it be all right if we turn the boat over and use it as a hut?'

History does not relate what occurred at this embarrassing moment, or how much of the story is apocryphal, but the term 'appropriate technology' must have been born on this day.

...........................................

*'On one occasion we found a child sitting alone in the relief camp crying. The doctor explained that she had just been told that her parents and brothers were all dead. She alone of her family had survived' (David Coulson's diary).*

One overseas government, to cite another example, has built a beautiful hospital on the Tana River in north-eastern Kenya. It has modern operating theatres and generators and all the equipment of a modern hospital. When it came to running it, however, there was not enough money to pay for the diesel to light it and operate the generators for power. The government's allowance of diesel for a whole year was 400 litres. The glittering equipment in the kitchens, laundry and theatre remained without light or power, so torches were used in the theatre, and the kitchen staff resorted to the old African way of cooking over a few stones outside on the ground. So much misplaced generosity is heart-breaking indeed.

This example also illustrates another lesson we have to learn. As already suggested, any project must allow for running costs over a long period and not just for capital expenditure. In arranging this it must be remembered that trade is better than aid, for trade brings employment in its wake and helps a country to stand on its own feet. Each and every project should be enabled eventually to support itself and become commercially viable. Where this can be achieved the local population do not feel that they are being saddled with the impossible task of keeping the project running in the future. With government help where necessary, and with the initial assistance of the aid organizations, it should be possible to make even hospitals a viable proposition, always provided that the technology is kept within reasonable bounds.

Lord Harris of High Cross, Director of the Institute of Economic Affairs, has written along these lines in an article entitled 'Small is Helpful', published in *The Times* in 1986. His theme is that wherever aid is applied, the smaller the project the more likely it is to succeed. The 'ground nut schemes' which were a feature of the 1950s and 1960s should be a thing of the past. Village projects and cottage industries are understood and appreciated, but huge enterprises involving large-scale movements of population, with all the associated problems, should be avoided wherever possible.

Kenya is probably representative of most of Africa in being faced with an exploding population, with little industrial development to sustain it and produce employment. It is to the village artisan, and the development of village life, that we should look to provide the much needed employment and the development of a better standard of living for the community as a whole.

These observations apply to any country in Africa which is making the transition from the old life to the new. They apply most strictly in Ethiopia. Much fertile land in Ethiopia could be developed and made fruitful, producing most of the food for its inhabitants, even with the ravages of drought. The planning and encouragement of peasant agriculture could save the day throughout the continent, but for this to happen a proper price policy encouraging full cultivation of staple crops is of primary importance. Farmers are not paid enough for their produce in most countries, and therefore lack incentive to produce more. A review of the price structure for primary products could thus be more important than aid.

*A turbanned priest processes through Lalibela during the annual Timket festival. The priests are getting older and few young men are joining the church. In the old days the church had land and was powerful. Now it has been stripped of its land and wealth. The present government is committed to eradicating all forms of religion.*

There are signs that this message is at last being heeded in Africa, and attention is being paid to the needs of the peasant farmer. This is all the more important since this is the one area where productivity could increase the fastest. A recent article from China states that wheat production is rising 12 per cent per year as a result of the activity of peasant farmers, making China now the world's biggest wheat producer. How was this achieved? Can we learn anything from this experience? It was not achieved by the conventional ideas of the water experts who have been preaching big dams, huge irrigation schemes and big everything else as the only way to agricultural growth. It was the result of giving the peasants the proper help and the proper incentive to allow them to produce more.

This is the crux of the aid situation. It is perfectly possible in most parts of Africa for the peasants to grow enough for their country's needs by increasing the yields per acre. This will be a much happier answer than importing subsidized food, which tends to depress the local market. It is a stark fact that the peasants work hard for about one hundred days a year while planting and harvesting, and then hardly at all for the other two hundred and sixty-five days. This is not their fault as there is practically nothing else for them to do. But big increases in rural production would flow from discovering how to fill the hours of those two hundred and sixty-five wasted days – for instance by growing a second crop for export. This in turn would circulate money in the rural areas and even spread to the towns which are the rural shopping centres.

Every African country could do four things to boost its agriculture and to rely less on foreign aid. First, remove all policies which work against the peasant farmer; the worst of these are price controls that reduce the return the farmer gets. Secondly the exchange rate of African currencies must be looked at since most of them are over-valued, tending to promote agricultural imports and depress agricultural exports. Thirdly, technological improvements such as those that have brought about the Green Revolution in India must be studied and, where practicable, introduced. The second generation of the miracle seeds that led to the greatly increased yields of staple crops in the Punjab are specifically intended for those parts of the world where the climate is bad and unreliable. Aid should be given to researching into the appropriate crops for each area, and for the purchase of seeds and fertilizer to be distributed in these areas.

Finally, governments and donors need to understand that the best investments are not the huge projects which, although carrying prestige, are wasteful. Such money as is available on this scale could be used more profitably for rural roads, village water, rural clinics and virtually anything which will make life in the bush more interesting and stimulating. People will stay in the rural areas and stop going

*(Opposite above) Beta Giorgis (the Church of St George, patron saint of Ethiopia) with its triple cruciform, one of Lalibela's twelfth-century rock-hewn churches. Seen here during the annual festival of Timket, this church can only be entered by a tunnel dug deep into the mountainside. Elsewhere in the world such churches would be mere monuments to a former glory. Here they continue to be strongholds of a living faith.*

*(Opposite below) A man carrying famine relief grain from Germany passes the Timket procession in Lalibela.*

to the towns once these facilities and amenities are improved and the standard of living goes up. At the moment if the peasant improves his productivity there is nothing to spend his money on.

Another problem which should be checked but which is outside the control of the poorer countries, is the subsidies given by the rich countries to their own farmers. When famine hits a country, then it is true that it needs all the imported food it can get. But too much of the produce of subsidized farming in North America and Europe is sent as aid to poor countries to keep the price of food cheap for the urban population, who are more ar iculate and therefore hold the major political power. The local farmer is impoverished by this, and imported food tends to become a way of life for the urban dwellers.

An increase in production can soon produce surpluses. But Africa is very short of crop storage facilities, and it is estimated that 40 per cent of what is produced goes to waste as a result of lack of storage. Recently both Kenya and Zimbabwe were faced with this problem with heavy rains approaching. The World Bank and other relief agencies came to the rescue and purchased the Zimbabwe crop and distributed it to Mozambique which was suffering a famine.

This action pinpoints the root of the famine problem. Often one country may experience plenty, while others that are in need cannot afford to buy their neighbour's surplus. Poverty and the inability, either on a national or personal level, to buy food is the intractable problem at the root of hunger. The increase of purchasing power, the initiation of new wealth, the purchase and distribution, as well as the storage, of local surpluses, are all areas in which aid could be successfully deployed.

I have cited the example of food aid, but such comments are equally applicable to other sectors of the economy. 1984 was the year of the great famine in large parts of Africa. The emotional response from the West was astonishingly generous, but this will only deal with the short-term problem, while the long-term problem will depend on the actions which we can and must take, here and now, in Africa. It is the responsibility of the independent African governments to plan to prevent disasters in the future. The remedies are simple, and yet they involve the supreme obstacle of people's attitudes, particularly the attitudes of those profiting from power. It is an immense task to alter these opinions and to instil the will to bring about change. No amount of aid, or even supervision, can overcome the apathy derived from economic failure, or the age-old custom of graft which more and more seems to be the accepted practice of the day.

These are hard judgements but no lover of Africa can shirk the truth as he sees it. In Africa we do not think about tomorrow. We are improvident, and this makes long-term planning difficult. The West is wondering why it should continue to support countries like Ethiopia, whose own government appears to put profits before human lives. How many millions are going to die before this is understood? Are we keeping people alive today for them to die next year? These are harsh questions, but they are being asked, and African governments need to give the

......................................................

*(Previous page) Periodically the procession stops and the priests gather on a ridge, flanking the route, to dance. Each priest holds a ceremonial staff and a sistrum, said to be the world's most ancient musical instrument.*

*Turbaned Christians carry their church 'tabots'—emblems of their faith, as they process through Lalibela. These tabots or tablets, made of stone, wood or gold and inscribed with the ten commandments, are brought out once a year during the great Timket festival. The oldest tabots of all date back to the time of Solomon and the Queen of Sheba. No layman may set eyes on the tabots, traditionally shrouded in colourful brocades.*

............................................

answers. Aid is growing less because these questions are being swept under the carpet and disillusionment is not being checked.

Our motivation and accountability need urgent attention if we are to expect the donor nations to continue to help. Better still we need to produce more and it is well within our powers to do so. I believe that there is a growing realization of these problems, and a growing wish to take responsible action and build truly independent nations. Once this has been fully digested there is no reason why we should not generate our own wealth rather than expect to live on other people's. Attitudes need to be expanded to encompass a national view, rather than limited to a personal, family or tribal perspective. For such changes to come about, Africans themselves must initiate and pursue them.

# CHAPTER ELEVEN

# THE BEST MEDICINE

.................................................

On Saturday mornings in the sixties and early seventies, I would take off from our farm on the slopes of Kilimanjaro and fly to Moshi some sixty-five miles away on the opposite side of the mountain. The loveliness of those mornings is with me still. Often the farm would be above the cloud. Looking down on a soft white blanket the horny backs of Namanga and Longido Mountains could be seen poking through like the ridged spines of insects. Looking up we would see the clear gleaming summit of Kilimanjaro dominating the huge landscape. It was difficult to believe its power and height, which appeared so dramatic from the surrounding plains. Its huge shoulders, often hidden as the mists rose, were 120 miles round. Its perfect volcanic shape and the glittering snow summit against the depths of blue sky gave this mountain and this place a unique character.

As I loaded the small aircraft with my surgical instruments I would look across the wide valley to Meru Mountain, its crater gaping darkly from its sun-drenched cliffs. It was a landscape for giants. No wonder the plans we made on that mountain were daring and huge, involving a continent. To relive those mornings, with the sun-filled air round our heads, is to re-open an old wound, for our farm became part of a government buy-out and in 1975 we were forced to leave and return to Nairobi. Yet we have been granted to live out some of those dreams and that is a great reward. I went home to the farm from there to Moshi every weekend to help build the Kilimanjaro Christian Medical Centre, which became the most modern hospital in Tanzania. It was also my task to prepare an extensive list of all the equipment and supplies required by the hospital, prepare tenders and order them. Later I undertook one day a week of surgery at the hospital until 1975.

The flight to Moshi began at 6,300 feet above sea level, while the take off runway ran down between the fields of wheat on our farm in the direction of the Amboseli National Park some 2,000 feet below. The contrasts in the environment were plain to see and demonstrated vividly the effect of altitude. Starting from the snow and glaciers of the top 4,000 feet of Kilimanjaro, there came the barren alpine desert of rocks, scree and heath, which in turn stretched down to the forest which began around 10,000 feet above sea level. This indigenous forest was wrapped like a green belt around the mountain and was full of elephant, buffalo, colobus monkeys and many other varieties of game. Then came the farming belt and finally the hot dry semi-desert of Amboseli, the National Park at the foot of the mountain. From the air this panorama of different varieties of country could be taken in at a glance, and it was an education in both the potential and constraints of the agricultural terrain. The effects of temperature, rainfall and soil were clear as I flew on round the west side of the mountain and finally over the fertile southern flank occupied by the progressive Chagga tribe whose land is well developed and whose farms produce good coffee among other products.

Although my main task was medical at that time, I became increasingly interested in the subject of nutrition and therefore of food production. It was obvious that poor nutrition was the basis of poor health and it seemed to me that food must be a major priority, and could be seen as the best medicine in our catalogue of curative systems. It was finally the desperate drought and famine of 1984 which helped to crystallize my thinking about food production, and I became interested in seeking ways to overcome the potential tragedy of ever growing famine in Africa. My interest in farming goes back thirty-five years to the time when Susan and I left the town and bought a small farm twenty miles out of suburban Nairobi. Our experiences there, despite our many mistakes, whetted our appetite for farming on a larger scale, and this is how we came to move to Kilimanjaro where we ran three farms. Two adjacent farms were at Ol Molog and one, a ranch in the lower country, was at the base of the mountain.

Fortunately for us, our amateur efforts were reinforced by a number of professional helpers, and slowly we began to learn about this most fascinating of all ways of life. Robin Ulyate, who married our daughter Janet, had farming in his blood. He was an outstanding man with machinery and had an innate sense of what could be done and what should be left well alone. He was born and bred in East Africa, and had learnt the art of improvisation to a high degree. His contribution to our farming efforts was very substantial. Hugo, our younger son, read agriculture at university and came back from Wye Agricultural College to farm in Africa. He, too, was a great help to Susan who bore the main brunt of developing our farming ventures while I was largely engaged in my medical work. Hugo built up a prime dairy herd for us and it was one of the most valuable assets we left to Tanzania in 1975. Only at weekends was I able to watch the farming process and take part in a minor way in the constructive work of developing the land.

It was an immensely satisfying time and seemed to require every talent we could muster. All our four children have had the privilege of being brought up in the wide open expanses of an African farm and know that feeling of being close to nature. Despite the frustrations, the vagaries of the weather and the often critical periods of financial tightrope walking, the overall feeling of well-being and satisfaction easily outweighed the hazards and difficulties we encountered.

When our farms in Tanzania became part of a government buy-out scheme, Robin and Janet started a similar farming exercise in Kenya and pioneered a new area drawing on the experience they had gained in Tanzania. Hugo, after a year as a farm

*(Previous page) 'We had a farm in Tanzania on the western slopes of Mount Kilimanjaro, some of the most fertile land in Africa. Above the farm was a belt of indigenous forest full of elephant, buffalo, leopard and colobus monkeys. Below was the hot, dry, semi-desert of Amboseli, the National Park at the foot of the mountain.'*

manager in Brazil, returned to rent a sizeable piece of land next to Robin in Maasailand, 120 miles west of Nairobi. They have both made a well-earned success of these ventures, while Susan and I have been able to visit and watch this next generation struggle with and enjoy the experience of developing a farm in Africa.

It is our continuing interest in the farming world that has led me recently to start an organization which aims to assist in the challenging field of agricultural development in Africa. FARM, the Food and Agricultural Research Mission, was launched early in 1986, and is currently going through the initial stages of registration and fund-raising. In the drive to help feed Africa, it is FARM's plan to concentrate its efforts on peasant agriculture, and in the dry areas to experiment with highly bred camels for milk production. FARM will cooperate with other aid schemes as far as possible, utilizing such resources as are already there. Examples will be drawn from other parts of Africa and the knowledge gained from such experience will be disseminated in handbooks. Zimbabwe, for instance, has much to teach other countries with a peasant farming policy which could revolutionize production all over Africa.

It might seem superfluous to start yet another organization when there are already so many in the field. Yet I am a believer in multiplicity of action leading to the same goal. The matter is so urgent that every small contribution can be of use in bringing about the 'green revolution' in Africa which everyone wants to see. The recent overwhelming success of Band Aid, Live Aid and Sport Aid have demonstrated the willingness of the ordinary citizen to give to what is seen to be one of the great crises of our day. The generous reaction of the public, and particularly its younger members, to these campaigns has been both astonishing and heartwarming. The emotional appeal to save people from starvation by donating food is a very strong one and entirely necessary in a crisis. That this needs to be followed by longer term action is also obvious if similar crises are to be avoided. There are strong reasons to believe that the crisis could be overcome within one generation; this has already been accomplished in India and is now in process in Indonesia. The easy transfer of technologies from India to Africa is unlikely, given their different circumstances, but nonetheless much can be learnt from their methods, above all in the use of improved seed.

Our exciting goal is thus an Africa able to feed its burgeoning population by the end of the century. FARM wants to see a green Africa by the year 2000. This is accepted as possible by most experts, though there are naturally some strong provisos. The most important among these will be the political will of African governments to bring about the necessary policy changes. There are many other essential factors, but none of them are insuperable. Among them is the need to strengthen the infrastructure in agriculture because when this element falters, the farmer, however expert, does not have the backing to store, transport and market his produce. Credit schemes, the training of extension workers, are other essential ingredients to get the agricultural industry properly functioning.

Following the appalling drought and famine of 1984, good harvests of certain crops, notably in Zimbabwe and Kenya, have highlighted the problem of farming surpluses. People cannot afford to buy food, having traditionally always grown food and not bought it. At the same time governments cannot afford to buy other countries' surpluses. Poverty can thus be seen to be the real crux of the matter, for any drive to increase food production will be largely ineffective, unless there is someone to buy the food made available. Food aid by itself is often counterproduc-

tive because it tends to upset the local market. During the Ethiopian famine, there were often markets selling food situated alongside famine camps. The overriding problem was that the purchasing power of the peasantry had declined to almost nothing.

The essential problem is thus that of creating new wealth in the developing countries, particularly in those which are not oil producing. How is this to be done? It would appear that agriculture possesses the greatest potential for the coming generation. Rural development will depend on it, though there will be an associated need for secondary industry based on agricultural requirements in machinery, buildings and transport. As long as prices for agricultural produce are low, storage inadequate, transport expensive and the middle man taking an unfair proportion of the profits, the peasant will only produce what he needs for himself and his family. But given proper incentives there is ample evidence that peasant food production can be increased.

Above all these issues stands the horrific spectre of an ever increasing population whose dangers have already been mentioned in previous chapters. As this population expands faster than the economy the standard of living will continue to depreciate. Western experience shows that it is prosperity which leads to reduction in the birth rate: once again poverty can be seen to be the underlying cause of the problem. Even today the world produces enough food to give every man, woman and child a 3,000-calorie daily diet. Its unequal distribution is the result simply of the complications of world trade and the inadequate purchasing power of the poorer sections of the community.

With food, or the lack of it, marches the problem of water. Despite the 'Decade of Water' and many other campaigns to bring clean drinking water to the villages of the world, there is still a very long way to go. Piped water is an expensive luxury, but clean drinking water would improve health more than any other single factor. So many diseases are water borne, and the introduction of clean potable water can have a revolutionary effect on health, as was seen in Western countries in the middle of the last century. Statistics for that period show beyond doubt that it was public health measures – such as better housing, better nutrition and better sanitation, as well as cleaner water – that played the major part in improving the general health of the population. We are now so impressed by the brilliant medical inventions and technology of the day that we forget the immense step forward which occurred through improved public health measures long before immunization, antibiotics, transplants and the other miracles of modern medicine were introduced. For us in the developing world the appeal of modern drugs and other glamorous adjuncts of modern medicine tends to obscure what really needs to be done first. Without the revolution in public health, modern therapy will be largely wasted.

Above all nutrition – in simple terms food – hand in hand with clean water, has

......................................

*(Previous page) 'Looking up from the farm we would see the gleaming summit of Kilimanjaro.' Seen here from the south west, Kilimanjaro is the highest mountain in Africa (19,340 feet). It was once given as a birthday present by Queen Victoria to the Kaiser, her nephew. This explains the kink in the otherwise straight border between Kenya and Tanzania. The main crater pictured here is known to the local Chagga people as 'Kibo', meaning 'snow'.*

the largest role to play in the improvement of health, and it is to the millions of small peasant holdings that we must look for an adequate supply. This is the level at which help is most urgently needed, and at which FARM plans to offer assistance.

To research our first project to improve peasant farming David Campbell, FARM's Executive Director, and I set off recently into Ukambani and the Yatta plateau south east of Nairobi. One of FARM's initial projects is the improvement of the stock of goats. If on smaller plots a highly productive goat could be kept instead of cattle, who consume so much more, a family could have enough milk for itself. With this in mind FARM is hoping to start the breeding of milk goats, and we were setting off to visit a goat-breeding station which had been set up near Kitui by a Catholic mission. In charge was Patrick Campbell, an old Africa hand and an experienced cattle man. He and his Mkamba wife live in simple style on the outskirts of Kitui.

To reach the mission we had to pass through the busy and untidy little town of Machakos. It was market day, and the brilliant colours of the women's khangas made a crazy kaleidoscope with the red tomatoes, the green herbs and cabbages, the beads and cloth which were on sale at the small stalls set up for the day. Chickens tied by their legs squawked anxiously on the sidelines, and goats of every colour and shape strode ostentatiously about cleaning up the rubbish and enjoying the warm sun and the activity. We drove carefully through the mêlée. Buses and matatus were blowing their horns to attract passengers, and the red dust rose in clouds as the crowd moved about the central market place. A row of small shops lined the road and I saw a board advertising 'Heart Specialist, Cures for all Diseases, Herbalist', but the curtained window showed none of these attractive wares.

We drove on into the country. The road wound through low hills and small plots and villages with some houses encouragingly marked 'Hoteli'. It was difficult to imagine how the people lived, for the maize in the small patches was shrivelled after three months of dry weather, and there remained another two months before rain could be expected. We were told, however, that money came into this area through the number of its menfolk employed in the police and the army. Small plots of cowpeas and banana palms alternated with the maize, and in the centre of a plot would be a square house made of plastered mud with a tin roof. There were a few desiccated gum trees and acacia thorn but the red soil looked exhausted and the trees red with dust.

At last we crossed the Athi River which was flowing fast and deep, and from there we climbed some 800 feet to the top of the Yatta plateau. Here the land seemed even drier and more exhausted than in the low country. Here and there a wispy patch of grass was being grazed by thin and listless cattle. There was little evidence of growing crops, and, not surprisingly, this area often has to resort to government famine relief. Even so this does not seem to restrict the increase in the population; we passed three secondary schools at lunch time, full of children playing in the courtyard and milling all over the road. I could not help but wonder what the future held for these children. The rural development was negligible, some villages not even having a football pitch. Where will they find employment? How will they be supported by this land? There did not seem to be any immediate answers, and the misery of extreme boredom seemed likely to be their fate.

We reached the project by noon; situated alongside, and surrounded by a fence of cactus, was the farmhouse of our friend Patrick Campbell. Invited in, we found an interior simply furnished with a table and three chairs. Some books on farming

*Small holdings in the Fort Hall/Nyeri district in the highlands east of the Aberdare Mountains. This land is some of the most fertile in Kenya. The brighter patches of green are tea plantations.*

...............................................

lay around and a few pictures were hung rather high on the walls. Patrick farms 6,000 acres for the mission and he also runs a training centre teaching local people how to farm sheep and goats. At the centre are buildings and accommodation for visiting students. The farmers come to the school for a few days and learn animal care. The stall-feeding of goats and sheep – a way of avoiding the destructive habits of goats when left to forage for themselves – is also taught. This is a new idea for Wakamba farmers, although their neighbours, the Kikuyu, have stall-fed cattle for a long time. In this way grazing will be controlled and erosion avoided. At the end of the course the best farmers are encouraged to buy male goats to upgrade their stock. Yet the herd comprises only 1,000 animals and therefore falls far short of demand.

It is FARM's hope to build on this project which is now run on a shoestring, injecting funds which could add to the supply of goats and increase the Centre's facilities. The present stock consists of pure white Galla goats. They are not very big and have short hair. Crossed with Swiss Toggenburg, without too much upgrading to avoid any loss of resistance to local diseases, they could provide greatly increased yields of milk and meat in this marginal farming area. The sheep are Dorper and seem to thrive in the arid rocky surroundings. Patrick runs his herds on a controlled grazing system. There is no fencing for this, as the animals are herded by men and brought in during the noonday heat to water; they will lie in the shade of a gum tree until the sun lowers and the air cools. It is this central watering system which is restricting the use of the grazing available in the farther parts of the farm. Perhaps FARM will be able to contribute to this expansion of the watering system and thereby add a huge area for the grazing of increased herds.

Altogether this seemed an ideal place to start the project for goats. There was a sound scheme already in existence on which we could build, and that evening David Campbell and I came away well pleased with what we had seen.

Today we see a new wave of enthusiasm for the protection of our environment. This is very timely, though also very late in the day. The march southward of the Sahara desert is just one example of a frightening phenomenon which is going to take all the ingenuity of man to stop, backed by a formidable sum of money. The deforestation of large areas of indigenous forest and bush is producing a growing threat of further deserts and accompanying erosion on a large scale. In Ethiopia appalling statistics are available. Fifty years ago 60 per cent of the land was forested, now only 3 per cent of the land is forest. The insistence by many governments and organizations that more trees be planted is now just beginning to be heard and acted on. It is perilously late. The high price of charcoal has directly led to vast tracts of land being denuded of their natural covering of forest and bush, leaving the ground bare to the ravages of the sun, wind and tropical rain. An attempt to control or stop this trade is now being undertaken. Flying over the forests today one can see how thin they are becoming and how the line of the forest is receding higher and higher up the hills. The women have to go further and further to find the firewood they need for cooking, and it is a common sight to see them returning to their homes carrying heavy loads of wood on their backs after long expeditions into the bush and forest.

The problems facing any farming community are legion. Even if one sets aside the vagaries of the weather which are a major factor in any farming enterprise, there are other hazards which can mean the success or failure of a crop or enterprise. The production of cattle for the meat market for instance, requires the infrastructure of a veterinary service and probably an artificial insemination service also. Both services are beginning to fail in Africa, often for lack of funds for petrol, or lack of medicines and personnel. The artificial insemination service in Kenya for instance, which used splendid imported bulls and only charged one Kenyan shilling for the service of a cow, even if it took many shots to produce a pregnancy, is now in disrepair in many places and unable to operate. If from the beginning a more realistic sum had been charged for their services, and the original aid had been set up as an on-going commercial concern, they could now afford the necessary motorbike or Land Rover and the necessary fuel to keep the operation in existence.

The availability of land, and the system of land tenure, must be one of the most important factors influencing agriculture. Historically in England the system of primogeniture, the inheritance by the eldest son of the whole property, saved English farming land from fragmentation and preserved the country's agriculture. In Africa no such system existed, and in many areas the land became impossibly dispersed between rival wives and numerous sons until it has become difficult for the smaller plots to support one family. After the Mau Mau the colonial government made a great effort to give individual title to much of the land in Kenya, in particular among the Kikuyu, and the rule of primogeniture is actively encouraged. This has done something to stem the fragmentation of the land, and the flourishing farms of Kikuyuland and Kisii prove the point. Recently individual title has been given to much of Maasailand with a less successful result. Here individuals attracted by cash are being tempted to sell or rent their land to the game lodges which are proliferating, and even to would-be farmers from other tribes, endangering the pastoral way of life. Even more recently the renting of land, although successful in the main, could become a danger to the fertility of the soil through the newly gazetted 'guaranteed minimum return'. Under this scheme the government guarantees to pay the farmer a set minimum for his crop thus relieving him of the enormous risk involved in arable farming. It will be necessary to instal strict supervision of any such assistance to farmers to prevent exploitation of the soil.

In other parts of the world state ownership has killed the incentive to produce a flourishing agriculture, and it is hoped that the introduction of individual ownership, together with the controls provided by government, will produce the right background for a developing agriculture in Africa. But there are many areas where antique systems still prevail and tribal lands need modernizing.

In the desert areas of northern Kenya nomadic tribes still continue their traditional way of life. Modern policy is to settle them in villages, and to change their way of life to that of the agriculturalist. Although such a move would theoretically bring some benefits to the people, such as schools, health centres and other village amenities, it is unlikely that the land would sustain concentrations of population, and even more unlikely that the tribes themselves would be able and prepared to adapt. To help them sustain their present way of life FARM has initiated a project to help develop the livestock of the desert tribes by upgrading the camels and cattle so that they can support the existing population.

Preparing the ground for our project, David Campbell and I recently drove north in a Land Rover to the Laikipia plains where Jasper Evans, a rancher, has bred camels for many years. We drove north through Nyaharuru and Rumuruti and came out on the beautiful green plains of Laikipia. The grass was waving kneehigh, following a good rainy season. Never had I seen the country so lush and fertile, with wild flowers dancing in the long grass.

Jasper's ranch consists of some 35,000 acres of what is usually hard dry pasture and bush. On this land he has 2,000 head of cattle, 2,000 goats and sheep and 450 camels. It was to set up a project with some of the camels that we were visiting this remote area. The object of the project was to establish whether, with regular milking and feeding with forage, camels would give more milk. For if, with care and these methods, the milk production of camels could be increased, then even one camel could feed a family. The camel also has the advantage of being able to go for three weeks without water, and his large padded feet do not erode the soil as do the cloven hooves of cattle.

We drove slowly through a yard of old rusting machinery, up to the house which was of wood, with an iron roof. One enters most Kenya houses through the verandah or the kitchen. On this occasion we crossed the verandah on which was kept a supply of veterinary drugs, bottles, old hats, and saddles. On the floor were dog baskets and blankets. The many dogs of the house milled round us as we entered, giving us a welcome. Inside the house comfortable chaos greeted us. The living room was full of books, stray papers and tumbledown chairs. The books –

*Deforestation of large areas of indigenous forest and bush is producing erosion problems on a frightening scale. This photograph shows a typical wash-away near Rongai in Kenya caused by deforestation.*

......................................................

about birds, flowers, cattle, animals – all reflected the immense knowledge of the country and the life in it that Jasper and his wife, Jill, have assimilated. To crown this multiplicity of things the walls were hung with gentle elegant watercolours, painted by Jill, of the magnificent landscapes among which they lived.

After a welcome farm lunch we retired with Jasper to his office to discuss our plans. He is a small man with startlingly blue eyes which, like those of a sailor, reflect the great distances with which he is familiar. Here in his office another mêlée of books, farm records, drugs, seeds and dogs greeted us. We planned together to experiment with fifty-four camels to start with. These would be selected from among his Somali, Turkana and crossbred stock, making a cross selection. In the preliminary stage we planned to milk these animals regularly and plant forage crops down by the river for the next stage of the experiment. So far the regular milking by two Turkana, one on either side of the camel, had added another two litres per animal to their milk production. The milk was being recorded; the crops of sorghum, wild beans, and elephant grass had been planted, and the night bomas of thorn were being built. Lion, leopard and cheetah prey upon the herds if they are not secured into thorn bomas at night. Elephants have smashed the fences, so the land is largely unfenced and the herds are guarded by Turkana, and returned to base at night, or to a thorn boma set up in the far parts of the ranch near some water supply.

213

We visited an outlying borehole and drove round parts of this flat open country. Rocky hills broke the skyline, and small valleys ending in sand rivers were studded with thorn bush. Jasper had built dams, which after five hard years of drought were full again. The big sky dominated all things, and as we turned home the sun fell below the flat edge of the earth leaving a trail of orange fire to challenge the oncoming night.

Besides improving the livestock which support the dry areas, covering two thirds of Kenya, FARM foresees a pattern of rural development in which peasant farms all over the country will be fostered by improved roads, better marketing facilities, and the proper storage for surpluses. Prompt payment for crops and increased prices will no doubt increase production, but at the expense of the urban poor. The unemployed who have lost touch with the land, and who live in slum conditions round the big towns, are another problem and will somehow need to be fed. Government subsidized prices could be a first step in bringing them relief, and higher production could in the long run mean cheaper food. Some problems are for solving and some, on the other hand, have to be lived with. Whichever the problem it seems there is also room for hope that the coming years will see an increase in prosperity.

In the days when we farmed some of the most fertile land in Africa on Kilimanjaro, I would return to Nairobi on a Monday morning, flying over the soda lake of Amboseli and up across the Maasai plain with its miles of scrub and bush often shrouded in mist. It was then that the size of Africa and the size of the problem would become visible. Yet perhaps it is the size that is not only the problem, but also the cure. For here is space, so lacking in other countries, and given the will and the money these waterless plains could come to life and provide for the new life of the developing continent.

*In the desert areas of northern Kenya the nomads still pursue their traditional way of life. FARM has initiated a project to help these people upgrade their livestock. Rendille warriors are seen here drawing water from a well at Ilaut for their animals. These wells are known as singing wells because the warriors form a human chain to pass the water, chanting rhythmically as they pass the buckets one to another.*

# CHAPTER TWELVE

# THE PATH WINDS UPWARDS

...............................................

A frica, the bewitching continent, lies between East and West and is shaped like a question mark. Its very name seems to conjure up a host of intangible emotions and an aura of unsolved mysteries. For those who live and work in Africa the spell of its mysteries and spaces lasts a lifetime. Africa, after centuries of relative isolation, is emerging to take its place in a world dominated by technical advance. The giant is waking and stretching his limbs and we all wait to see how he will use his strength and his resources. At the moment he seems bewildered and distraught, desperately trying to find his way through a maze of contradictory paths. It is an uncomfortable time, as must be expected, for uncertainty is dominant, and no one can tell where the next upheaval will occur. In politics, in education, in agriculture, in health and population, in all stratas of society huge changes are taking place. The stirrings of a new society and civilization can be detected, although it is too early in the moulding process for its final guise to be foretold. East does meet West in Africa. North too meets South. What will emerge from these historic meetings?

Within the framework of this continent there live many people seemingly unaffected as yet by the turmoil around them. They may be subconsciously beginning to feel the first shock waves but in day to day life they are largely unaware of the developments approaching. Many people still live as their forefathers did, and in the same place. It is this strange contrast which fascinates the country's increasing number of visitors who seem to sense that unless they see Africa today, it will be changed tomorrow beyond recognition. In its cities the same restlessness and ferment can be seen as in other cities of the world, but thirty miles or so from the towns you find yourself back in the Stone Age. It is this amazing mixture which intrigues us, and when this is added to the spaciousness and beauty of the landscape and the charm and diversity of its people we have ingredients which are both unique and provocative.

Over the last forty years I have experienced and observed the upheavals, watched the great developments and participated in some of the life, while helping to found and develop a medical institution. Now as I relinquish the direction of AMREF I look back with nostalgia to the early days of its inception. They were exhilarating times, when the whole world appeared to be at our feet. It seemed possible then to change the world, to create new conditions, to solve old problems, to carve out new lives. At the time it felt good and right to bring science and the Western way of life to Africa. We imagined that our skills and dreams would benefit this section of mankind. Forty years later I am ready to offer it my doubt, my willingness for its people to express their essence, even in chaos if need be, so that Africa may emerge whole and fulfilled.

In those far-off days I would sit, with my two plastic surgeon friends, Sir Archibald McIndoe and Dr Tom Rees, on our farm on Kilimanjaro, and over a whisky we would lay our exciting plans for the future. The land below the verandah turned abruptly into rolling wheatfields newly cultivated from raw bush, then it fell two thousand feet into the semi-desert of Lake Amboseli, where the distances melted away into changing colours for a hundred miles up into Kenya. The nights were crisp and cold, and a log fire would be burning.

Being three plastic surgeons our first project was for a plastic unit to deal with the mass of trauma so evident at the time. Burns, car accidents, animal wounds and the ravages of untreated disease were among the most urgent cases we saw in need of reconstructive surgery. Immediately after the war, however, the donor countries were poor, and did not respond to the idea of building in the Third World. It was then, by force of necessity, that I turned my mind to flying. If we could not build a unit, then I would try taking specialist skills out to the bush hospitals. I learnt to fly and in my Piper Tripacer began answering emergency calls and visiting mission hospitals in the bush. From this grew the need for radio communication, and the radio network of the Flying Doctor Service was set up. Gradually more aircraft were added to the fleet and the gift of a twin engined Aztec gave us a range which covered East Africa.

In those days one had only to think of an idea to be able to put it into operation. Nowadays one of the biggest obstructions to any development project in Africa or overseas is weight of the bureaucracy with which we have to deal. It is a serious deterrent to development, and a costly burden on government. No doubt the need for employment keeps it at its present level, but it is a hindrance to all but the most brave and determined.

AMREF now has around 400 men and women working from headquarters in Nairobi, to operate forty-seven projects in five different countries. Even as far off as Botswana there is a daughter organization, the 'Flying Mission', which provides a Flying Doctor Service for the whole of the Kalahari desert and the rest of Botswana. It has three aeroplanes and five pilot mechanics, and doctors and nurses as well. This organization was designed on the East African model, and now flies more than 1,300 hours a year over those arid and empty spaces.

The last twenty-five years in Africa have seen a gradual inclusion of African staff into every side of life and work in Kenya. AMREF is no exception, and we have men and women at the middle level who are outstanding in skills and calibre. They represent a new cadre growing up in the country, and their quality and determination is going to bring about changes in Kenya that can only be for the better. I am proud to know many of them through AMREF, and their existence reaffirms my belief that the future Africa is coming alive, and in strength.

The cataclysmic famines of the last ten years have brought about a serious mood among politicians all over Africa. No longer are they so absorbed with their power, position and wealth. They have been to the brink and come back to give more emphasis to agriculture and more support to the peasant and the rural economies of their countries. This is a marked advance which has come directly out of the tragedy of the famine years. The path will continue to be upward for a long time yet but because of the calibre of the generations now taking part in the struggle, it will be a path of achievement.

So it is good to begin again. 'Out of Africa there is always something new.' I was talking recently to an old African friend of mine who is from Tanzania, and has known years of struggle in running an art gallery outside Nairobi. 'The years of independence are at an end,' he said, 'and the years of interdependence are beginning.' If such interdependence comes about a great leap forward in development will take place, for many enthusiastic black, white and brown people exist, who if given the chance would gladly devote their lives to building Africa. Africa is no man's debtor. It gives again and again the sun and air, the warmth and spaces, the charm of its many peoples, the mystery of many beginnings, and above all a life of significant meaning.

Laurens van der Post tells a story: There was a bushman who was visited by three daughters of the gods. He chose the most beautiful and married her. She brought with her a box, with strict instructions that this was her gift to the bushman, but that he must never, under any circumstances, look into the box. Of course curiosity finally overcame him and he opened the box; there was nothing inside. The girl immediately disappeared and never returned. Thus he was punished, not because he disobeyed and looked into the box, but because he could not see what was inside; he could not see the gifts that she had brought.

The reality which ancient man saw and expressed to the world of his day is still present with us. It is woven into the reality of the present. As we look into the treasure box of Africa we can see its richness shining through the myriad threads of present-day life, illuminating our reality with the originality and inspiration of the early soul of man.

# Glossary

M = *medical term*

**anaphylactic shock** (M) hypersensitivity of tissues to second dose of antidote

**autoclave** apparatus for sterilizing instruments and dressings by high pressure steam

**boma** thorn or other enclosure for protecting livestock or dwellings

**buibui** black garment worn by Swahili women leaving only their eyes uncovered

**dura** (M) membrane covering the brain

**eclampsia** (M) a kind of convulsion caused by toxaemia to which pregnant women are liable

**gari** Swahili name for vehicle

**hydatid disease** (M) Echinococcus Granulosus. A type of tape worm which gives rise to cysts in the liver and other parts of the body (*see* pp. 44–53)

**jihazi** type of dhow or Swahili sailing boat

**jini** Swahili and Arab name for a spirit or spirits, genie or djinn

**kala-azar** (M) a tropical disease caused by bite of sand fly

**Kamba** see Mkamba

**kikoi** cotton wrap around cloth worn by Swahili men on East African coast

**kraal** group of huts enclosed by a fence; enclosure for cattle or sheep

**Mbogo and Mkomo trees** indigenous trees near East African coast

**manyatta** Maasai village or collection of houses

**Mkamba** African tribe living East of Nairobi (plural Wakamba)

**moran/morani** Maasai warrior or warriors

**omobari** a traditional surgeon healer from Kisii who specializes in craniotomies (skull surgery)

**panga** Swahili for a type of hatchet commonly used in Africa for cutting wood

**pepo** Swahili word meaning a spirit (or wind)

**Ras** an Ethiopian nobleman

**Rohani** Swahili word meaning good spirit

**rungu** Swahili word meaning a club

**shamba** Swahili word meaning a garden or allotment

**Shetani** Swahili word meaning evil spirit

**shifta** Somali brigand

**Shoga** male prostitute in Swahili society

**Shukha** red cloth worn by Maasai

**simi** Swahili word meaning a short sword

**simsim** a legume which produces oil

**tabot** sacred Ethiopian tablet inscribed with the 10 commandments

**trephine** (M) surgical instrument for drilling hole in the skull

**Ukambani** tribal area east of Nairobi, home of the Kamba people (Wakamba)

# Note on AMREF

AMREF was formed with one simple objective, namely 'To improve the health of the people of Africa'. To achieve this it has a widespread programme which it has built up over the last thirty years. It is an independent international non-profit-making organization with its headquarters in Nairobi and is supported by national offices in the UK, USA, Germany, Sweden, Canada, Denmark, France and the Netherlands. There are some 420 people from nineteen countries working for the Foundation and its budget for 1987 is around £8 million, all of which has to be raised by the organization itself.

AMREF's emphasis is on grassroots projects in the rural community with the purpose of involving the community in safeguarding its own health. Public health and preventative measures are recognized as a priority although clinical services remain a major occupation. The programme includes family planning as part of a maternal and child health service. Departments of training, health behaviour and education, clinical services and research are backed by a series of support services which include a printing shop, a book distribution unit, a community health workers support unit, a Flying Doctor Service with extensive radio communications and a small fleet of light aircraft, and an environmental health unit. The administration and accounting offices have to service the ongoing projects in the field and supply the donors with reports and accounts.

Over the years AMREF has assembled a considerable body of experience, working in many different countries in collaboration with the national Ministries of Health. It has developed a consultancy service which has been called upon in countries as far afield as Swaziland and Mali. In its works, and in the distribution of its rural health series manuals, AMREF has had a ripple effect and shares its accumulated knowledge widely with other organizations. It is in official relationship with the World Health Organization and has undertaken consultancies for the World Bank and other international bodies.

This short description can only give readers a broad outline of what AMREF is trying to do. Woven into its texture are numerous personal stories of success and failure, triumph and frustration, interest and adventure which make up the daily life of the organization. Only a fraction of these have been recorded in this book which embodies only my own reminiscences and expresses a personal view. It is hoped that the many generous donors to AMREF will sense what they have created and that it will serve as a human record of three decades of endeavour in this field of health in a continent which is constantly changing.

# INDEX

Numbers in *italic* refer to pages on which captions appear

221